REAL-TIME STUDENT ASSESSMENT

REAL-TIME STUDENT ASSESSMENT

Meeting the Imperative for Improved Time to Degree, Closing the Opportunity Gap, and Assuring Student Competencies for 21st-Century Needs

Peggy L. Maki

Foreword by George D. Kuh

STERLING, VIRGINIA

Published by Stylus Publishing, LLC.
22883 Quicksilver Drive
Sterling, Virginia 20166-2102

Library of Congress Cataloging-in-Publication Data
Names: Maki, Peggy, author.
Title: Real-time student assessment: meeting the imperative for improved time to degree, closing the opportunity gap, and assuring student competencies for 21st-century needs/Peggy L. Maki.
Description: First edition. |
Sterling, Virginia : Stylus Publishing, LLC, 2017. |
Includes bibliographical references and index.
Identifiers: LCCN 2016034572 (print) |
LCCN 2016059180 (ebook) |
    ISBN 9781620364888 (pbk. : alk. paper) |
    ISBN 9781620364871 (cloth : alk. paper) |
    ISBN 9781620364895 (library networkable e-edition) |
    ISBN 9781620364901 (consumer e-edition) |
Subjects: LCSH: Universities and colleges–
United States–Evaluation. |
Education, Higher–United States–Evaluation. |
Educational evaluation–United States. |
Educational tests and measurements–United States.
Classification: LCC LB2331.63 .M25 2017 (print) |
LCC LB2331.63 (ebook) |
DDC 378.73–dc23
LC record available at https://lccn.loc.gov/2016034572

13-digit ISBN: 978-1-62036-487-1 (cloth)
13-digit ISBN: 978-1-62036-488-8 (paperback)
13-digit ISBN: 978-1-62036-489-5 (library networkable e-edition)
13-digit ISBN: 978-1-62036-490-1 (consumer e-edition)

Printed in the United States of America

All first editions printed on acid-free paper
that meets the American National Standards Institute
Z39-48 Standard.

First Edition, 2017

10   9   8   7   6   5   4   3   2   1

To my husband's enduring patience.

CONTENTS

Real-Time Assessment as Engaging Pedagogy

When it comes to enriching student learning, we are pretty confident about the following:

- Students learn what they study and practice.
- How effectively students learn is a function of the quality of effort they devote to educationally purposeful activities.
- Learning is deepened when students focus effort over an extended period of time to assignments, projects, and activities that are challenging and personally meaningful.
- The best and most persuasive evidence of what students know and can do is their actual performance as demonstrated through writing, oral presentations, performances, demonstrations, and so forth.
- The more practice students get in transferring and applying their learning to unscripted problems embedded in concrete situations (e.g., community service, internships, research, campus employment), the better prepared they are to use effectively what they know.
- Connecting and integrating different learning experiences inside and outside the classroom through ongoing structured reflection helps to deepen learning and creates a foundation for continuous lifelong learning that is highly prized by employers in all sectors (granted, there is not a lot of empirical evidence supporting this assertion, but the premise is conceptually persuasive).
- Across all these conditions, feedback—especially when it is prompt and focused on specific, clearly defined behaviors—is the most powerful tool teachers, coaches, mentors, advisers, and students themselves have at their disposal to improve performance.

In general, feedback is most effective when it is given in close temporal proximity to the demonstration of the particular behavior; the more specific the feedback, the better. There are exceptions, of course.

Given this backdrop, real-time assessment—when done well—is a very attractive, much-needed option because it provides actionable information about the extent to which the learning conditions listed earlier are enacted. Moreover, the data are available in a time frame that makes it possible for both students and faculty to modify their behavior with an eye toward achieving the intended outcomes.

Making Assessment Matter in Real Time

One of the reasons that student learning outcomes assessment has had a relatively modest impact in terms of improving teaching and learning is because the approaches used most frequently to document student accomplishment yield little in the way of actionable data (Kuh et al., 2015). Often the findings come from national or local surveys about the student experience or scores on standardized tests from small, random samples of students, with the results aggregated and reported at the institutional level usually several months after the fact. Thus, the data do not represent student performance in specific classes or in response to assignments crafted by individual faculty; unfortunate, considering that assignment design is an especially powerful way to improve student performance (Hutchings, Jankowski, & Schultz, 2016). Also, aggregated institution-level information often does not speak to issues that faculty and staff consider relevant for working with their students or point to what they personally can do to improve teaching and learning. Students themselves are often puzzled when they are given tests seemingly unrelated to their program of study and about which their teachers exhibit little confidence or enthusiasm.

Equally important, by the time results from traditional assessment approaches become available, a new academic term or year has begun, and faculty and students have moved on to a different set of academic expectations and challenges. In other words, the data that could inform and influence faculty and students to improve their performance come to the fore too late to be of consequence.

How can we obtain—*in real time*—information that can help advance the outcomes we desire?

Fortunately, this informative tome by Peggy L. Maki is just in time. As readers will discover, assessment professionals, campus leaders, national higher education association officers, and accreditors rightfully have high regard for Maki's expertise and perspective (count me among them!). Drawing on her vast, rich experience, Maki offers many instructive ideas illustrated with concrete examples about how to gather and use actionable information in real time about what students are and are not doing that will enable them to acquire and demonstrate the knowledge, proficiencies, and dispositions postsecondary institutions promise and employers expect of the twenty-first-century learner and worker.

As Maki explains, there are a variety of resources available that colleges and universities can adapt to collect and analyze information about the quality of student performance to inform faculty and students about the degree to which students' knowledge acquisition and proficiency in various areas are satisfactory. Harnessing technology appropriately is especially important to real-time assessment, especially for doing this work at scale. Maki devotes an entire chapter to describing various tools for this purpose and offers campus-based examples of how colleges and universities have adapted existing platforms for various purposes.

Of course, technology is an empty vessel if not driven by curricular and pedagogical priorities, and a clear understanding of how real-time assessment can contribute to the institution's educational mission as well as bring coherence to what many students experience as a fragmented program of study. Toward these ends, Maki presents a conceptual framework in the form of five core learner-centered commitments an institution must make to realize the benefits of real-time assessment for both faculty and students. Facilitating conditions such as widespread collaboration and alignment among program aims, institutional values, and desired outcomes are mindful of the properties common to strong performing, engaging institutions described in *Student Success in College: Creating Conditions That Matter* (Kuh, Kinzie, Schuh, Whitt, & Associates, 2005/2010) and *The Undergraduate Experience: Focusing Institutions on What Matters Most* (Felten, Gardner, Schroeder, Lambert, & Barefoot, 2016). For example, real-time assessment can be thought of as the classroom-specific equivalent of an institutional early warning system; a faculty or staff member spots a student who is struggling, alerts a member of the student support response team, and the team contacts the student to provide assistance.

After presenting a persuasive brief for real-time assessment and describing the necessary facilitating institutional conditions, Maki offers six principles to guide the implementation of real-time assessment:

1. Internally driven and motivated
2. Inclusive of internal stakeholders
3. Bolstered by collaboration that harnesses others' expertise and practices
4. Anchored in continuous reporting and interrogation of assessment results
5. Responsive to students' needs in the present tense
6. Valued by the institution

These principles are consistent with ideas expressed in other work promoting promising assessment practices (e.g., National Institute for Learning Outcomes Assessment, 2016b).

Real-Time Assessment as an Engaging Pedagogical Practice

No one is more sensitive than Maki to the skepticism many faculty members still have about the merits of assessment. She thoughtfully describes the rationale undergirding the 16 Valid Assessment of Learning in Undergraduate Education (VALUE) rubrics, developed by teams of faculty and assessment specialists (including Maki) from across the country to help gauge performance on a wide range of outcomes (from writing to integrative learning, quantitative literacy to teamwork) (Rhodes & Finley, 2013). These rubrics have been used in targeted courses offered by individual institutions as well as in proof-of-concept experiments across dozens of colleges and universities in multiple states. As Maki emphasizes, the VALUE rubrics as well as other locally developed tools and scoring guides to document authentic learning are most powerful when they are adapted to the respective campus's educational purposes and related circumstances as well as closely aligned with essential twenty-first-century proficiencies, such as those articulated in the Degree Qualifications Profile (Lumina Foundation, 2014a). She then explains how these frameworks can help faculty members more accurately evaluate and monitor the effectiveness of their teaching and student learning.

The ePortfolio is especially important for leveraging the pedagogical power of real-time assessment. Thanks to the groundbreaking work of Eynon and Gambino (in press) and their colleagues in the Connect to Learning (C2L) network, we now have authoritative guidance for how to ensure high-quality implementation of the ePortfolio process, what they call the Catalyst for Learning Framework. As a result, to my mind the field now has enough evidence to declare preparation of ePortfolios—when done well—as a high-impact practice, an experience that deepens learning and boosts the performance of all students, especially those from historically underserved groups (Finley & McNair, 2013; Kuh, 2008; Kuh, O'Donnell, & Reed, 2013). Indeed, it behooves those embarking on real-time assessment to become familiar with best practices in using ePortfolios along with the emerging extended educational transcript that is intended to augment the traditional academic transcript by documenting a wide and rich set of proficiencies students have acquired beyond the classroom (Matthews, Zanville, & Duncan, 2016). Doing so would likely make what students have learned and are able to do more transparent, understandable, and meaningful to faculty, staff, employers, and students themselves.

Thanks to Peggy Maki for leading the way into the world and much-needed work of real-time assessment. While acting in real time has many virtues, it is also important to remember that these are early times in our understanding and use of the frameworks and tools she has so ably sketched. We will surely learn more and get better at this kind of assessment as more institutions experiment with what Maki has urged and challenged us to do.

George D. Kuh
Senior Scholar, National Institute for Learning Outcomes Assessment
Chancellor's Professor of Higher Education Emeritus, Indiana University

ACKNOWLEDGMENTS

I express deep appreciation to the following contributors of examples and case studies that illustrate the principles of real-time student assessment. Their contributions represent the kinds of steadfast collaborative steps that increasingly engage constituencies across an institution in a continuous shared commitment to the equitable success of our currently enrolled students.

Auburn University, Alabama

Lesley E. Bartlett, Assistant Director, Office of University Writing, ePortfolio Project
James C. W. Truman, Assistant Director, Office of University Writing
Gary Wagoner, Associate Professor Emeritus, Department of Art and Art History

Bridgewater State University, Massachusetts

Amanda Barudin, Director of Fieldwork and Staff Associate for Counselor Education
Ruth Slotnick, Director of Assessment

Carlow University, Pennsylvania

August C. Delbert, Director of Assessment, Institutional Research, Effectiveness and Planning
Anne M. Candreva, Assistant Vice President, Institutional Research, Effectiveness and Planning

DePaul University, Illinois

Ruben D. Parra, Director, Office for Teaching, Learning and Assessment

Governors State University, Illinois

Amy V. Comparon, Director of Tutoring and Academic Support, Academic Resource Center

Ann M. Vendrely, Associate Provost and Associate Vice President of Academic Affairs

Aurelio M. Valente, Vice President of Student Affairs and Dean of Students

Guttman Community College, New York

Laura M. Gambino, Associate Dean for Assessment and Technology

Mass Bay Community College, Massachusetts

Jim Grenier, Director of Online Education

Middlesex Community College, Massachusetts

Peter Shea, Director, Office of Professional Development

Pearson

Kristen DiCerbo, Principal Research Scientist and Lead of the Center for Learning Science and Technology at Pearson

Salem State University, Massachusetts

Jeramie Silveira, Graduate Coordinator in Occupational Therapy and Faculty Assessment Fellow

Tidewater Community College, Virginia

Kellie Sorey, Associate Vice President for Academics, Academic Affairs

University of Central Oklahoma, Oklahoma

Cia Verschelden, Executive Director, Institutional Assessment

University of Nebraska–Lincoln, Nebraska

Amy Goodburn, Associate Vice Chancellor
Nancy Mitchell, Director of Undergraduate Education Programs

University of St. Augustine for Health Sciences, Florida

David J. Turbow, Assessment Coordinator, Office of Assessment and Institutional Research
Thomas P. Werner, Assistant Director, Flex DPT Program

Utah State University, Utah

Norman Jones, Professor of History and Chair, Utah Regents' General Education Task Force

I also express my gratitude to the following individuals, higher education organizations, foundations, publishers, assessment management systems, and developers of technology and online interactive games or simulations:

American Historical Association for permission to reprint its 2016 History Tuning Project: Discipline Core on pages 40–42, chapter 2.

Richard Arum, Professor of Sociology, New York University, for permission to quote from his 2014 coauthored *Chronicle of Higher Education* article with Josipa Roksa. "Let's ask more of our students—and of ourselves," page 3, introduction.

Association of American Colleges & Universities for permission to reprint (a) *Liberal Education and America's Promise* Essential Learning Outcomes, Figure 2.1, page 31, chapter 2 and (b) Appendix 2A, the Critical Thinking VALUE Rubric, pages 49–52 and Appendix 2B, the Integrative Learning VALUE Rubric, pages 53–57, chapter 2.

Carnegie Foundation for the Advancement of Teaching for permission to quote from Ernest Boyer in *Scholarship Reconsidered: Priorities of the Professoriate*. Princeton, New Jersey,1990, page 23, chapter 1.

Institute for Evidence-Based Change, Brad Phillips, president/CEO, for permission to synthesize the Tuning process described in *Tuning American Higher Education: The Process*, 2012, Encinitas, CA: Author, page 39, chapter 2.

Natasha Jankowski for permission to quote from a chapter coauthored with Jillian Kinzie,"Making Assessment Consequential: Organizing to Yield Results" in George Kuh and colleagues (2015) *Using Evidence of Student*

Learning to Improve Higher Education, San Francisco, CA: Jossey Bass on page 3, introduction.

Joel Kotkin for permission to quote from his 2010 article in *The Smithsonian*, "The Changing Demographics of America," on page 14, chapter 1.

George D. Kuh for permission to quote from his coauthored 2014 book, *Knowing What Students Know and Can Do: The Current State of Learning Outcomes in US Colleges and Universities*, Urbana, IL: National Institute for Learning Outcomes Assessment on page 3, introduction.

Lumina Foundation for permission to reprint (a) the DQP Spiderweb framework on page 36, chapter 2, and (b) the list of students' expected degree proficiencies under "The Use of Information Resources," on page 37, chapter 2, from the 2014 *Degree Qualifications Profile 2.0*. Indianapolis, IN: Author.

Mavi Interactive, LLC, Bora Aytun, president, for permission to reprint the Agent SureFire screenshot, Appendix A5.2, page 145, chapter 5.

Pearson, Kristen DiCerbo, principal research scientist and lead of the Center for Learning Science and Technology, for permission to reprint screenshot Figure A5.3, page 146, chapter 5.

Simformer, Sergey Menshchikov, chief executive officer, Simformer.com, for permission to reprint Simformer screenshot Figure A5.1, page 144, chapter 5.

Taskstream, for permission to reprint screenshots Figures 5.2, 5.3, and 5.4 from its Aqua assessment management system, pages 124 to 126, chapter 5.

Tk20, for permission to reprint screenshot Figure 5.1 from its assessment management system, page 123, chapter 5.

Western Interstate Commission for Higher Education for permission to (a) reprint Table 1.1. U.S. Public High School Enrollment (Grades 9–12) by Race/Ethnicity, page 16, chapter 1 from Prescott and Bransberger (2012) *Knocking at the College Door: Projections of High School Graduates*, Boulder, CO: Western Interstate Commission for Higher Education, page 16, chapter 1; and (b) to quote from Prescott and Bransberger in "Demography as Destiny: Policy Considerations in Enrollment Management," 2013 in Policy Insights. Boulder, CO: Western Interstate Commission for Higher Education, pages 24 and 26–27, chapter 1.

John Wiley & Sons Ltd for permission to quote from McCormick's chapter, "Swirling and Double-Dipping: New Patterns of Student Attendance and Their Implications for Higher Education" in *New Directions for Higher Education*. Hoboken, NJ: John Wiley & Sons, 2003, page 46, chapter 2.

I express my gratitude to John von Knorring for his steadfast support of and commitment to this work and the production team at Stylus for their editorial expertise.

INTRODUCTION

A sense of urgency underlies the genesis of this book: the need for colleges and universities to develop a chronologically comprehensive, real-time, on-the-ground assessment system. This living-in-the-present approach is now necessary to address equitably the learning needs and challenges of currently enrolled students as they progress toward attaining a high-quality degree. The time is now to reframe your current assessment commitment to benefit the students logging on or sitting right in front of you. The time is now—after more than 40 years of a national focus on assessment—for all institutions to advance and implement an internally motivated and driven learner-centered assessment commitment. Focused on each student's equitable progression toward achieving a high-quality degree, this comprehensive continuous commitment needs to take place in real time, beginning at students' point of matriculation, entry, or reentry, and continuing until point of graduation.

Real-time student assessment shifts from a delayed use of assessment results, often extended well beyond when student work is collected, scored, and analyzed, to an immediate synchronous use of assessment results to address continuously the range of obstacles or persistent challenges that students face as they progress toward a degree. Continuous assessment closes time gaps that exist between periodic assessment approaches or cycles of assessment—gaps that represent missed opportunities to (a) identify students who are struggling academically and (b) address in real time the kinds of obstacles they face. Real-time student assessment requires nimbleness—the ability to address academic challenges that currently enrolled students face as they learn. It becomes another on-time gauge of students' progress toward attaining a degree along with other gauges that institutions currently use. Among those are early alert programs that identify students at risk of underperforming, programs that predict the likelihood of students' success in a course based on their previous performance levels, and effective advising

1

practices that include recognizing students' immediate needs and directing them to appropriate institutional resources.

Real-time student assessment is not uncharted territory. Programs such as music, theater, and art and professional preparatory programs such as teacher education and nursing, for example, have long integrated this continuous assessment approach into their curricula. The foundation of competency-based programs and degrees also rests on chronologically assessing students' performance toward mastery-level achievement. A small set of institutions, notably exemplified by Alverno College in its "assessment-as-learning process" (Alverno College, n.d.) continuously assesses its students' learning. In the case of Alverno College, each student's diagnostic digital portfolio provides the institution and its programs, as well as currently enrolled students, with actionable real-time assessment results. In recent years, several large-scale higher education consortia have been formed, such as the University Innovation Alliance (UIA), consisting of 11 large research universities focused on closing achievement gaps and graduation rates among students from all social and ethnic backgrounds. Besides recognizing the need to reform conventional educational practices to better serve students, these institutions also recognize the need to remain informed about and respond on time to students' academic and often personal needs. Real-time assessment results identify patterns of underperformance that need to be addressed through timely interventions for enrolled students.

What drives assessment in all of these examples is an internal need to know continuously how well students are progressing toward achievement of agreed-upon high-quality exit-level program and degree outcomes. These examples illustrate the assessment commitment that is now necessary across all of our institutions: an efficacious learner-centered assessment system that operates in the present tense, is internally motivated and driven, and values the nimble use of assessment results to advance all currently enrolled students to achieve a high-quality degree. However, these examples do not represent the assessment norm across our colleges and universities.

Achievement of Assessment's Purpose: Measurable Improvement of Student Learning

We all hoped assessment would measurably improve graduation rates to close opportunity gaps across historically underrepresented students. This has not been achieved across all of our institutions. Overall, using assessment results to redesign or innovate pedagogy and instructional methods is not our strong suit, even though it is the action-oriented purpose of the commitment. Indeed, the 2014 National Institute for Learning Outcomes

Assessment's (NILOA's) report on results of its 2013 survey of institutional assessment practices concludes that

> most institutions still need to find ways to use student learning outcomes results more effectively to improve teaching and learning. Although using assessment evidence appears to be increasing, it is not nearly as pervasive as it must be to guide institutional actions that will improve student outcomes. This is by far the most disappointing finding from the 2013 survey. (Kuh, Jankowski, Ikenberry, & Kinzie, 2014, p. 35)

Unfortunately, that finding is echoed in periodic surveys of institutions' assessment practices. Being able to act on assessment results remains a challenge, as a provost describes in the NILOA report: "Many faculty struggle with determining how to conduct a proper assessment and then how to use the results, and many of the disciplinary meetings are very broad and not specific in this regard" (Kuh et al., 2014, p. 28). More recently, Kinzie and Jankowski (2015) identify that the aim of assessment still remains largely unmet:

> Although more assessment evidence is available on campuses than ever before, information is not as widely shared as it should be and using it to guide institutional actions toward improving student outcomes is not nearly as pervasive as it could be. (p. 121)

Calling on institutions to become "more serious" about assessment, Arum and Roksa (2014) describe current commitments as "half-hearted compliance exercises," further saying that

> We have too often responded to accreditors' demands to demonstrate learning outcomes through half-hearted compliance exercises, which were focused on little more than satisfying visiting evaluation teams and achieving a passing grade that would keep accreditors at bay for another five years. It's the kind of approach to an assignment that, before grade inflation, we would not accept from our students. Instead, we should approach learning assessment with the same rigor that we ask of our students in their coursework.

Stated directly, the assessment status quo is not fulfilling its primary purpose: to improve our students' learning measurably.

For many institutions, assessment still remains solely an externally driven requirement—a response to outsiders' need for data, not an internally driven concurrent commitment to currently enrolled students' equitable long-term success. Some campus leaders, deans, department chairs, and faculty still confess that if it were not for regional, specialized, or national accreditation, their institutions and programs simply would not undertake this burdensome work. Reflective of a reactive attitude toward assessment are the following statements: "There is nothing we can do about it. It is here to stay." "We just have to do it." "We have to get ready for reaccreditation in the next two years, so gear up assessment now." A reductionist description of what faculty need to do is often presented to appease resistors: "We only need to give them exit-level results, so just give them assessment results from the capstone—that should do it." Interpreting and using results at the end of our students' journey may serve the needs of external stakeholders, but it does not serve the needs of those students on the path to graduation.

Understanding that the purpose of assessment is to improve student learning, many institutions earnestly work and have worked to achieve that aim, directing programs to establish and follow a multiyear assessment plan that explicitly plots when and how each of its learning outcomes will be assessed. On many campuses, an assessment cycle focused on just one or a small set of outcomes may take a year or more to complete. Interpretation of results and discussions about ways to improve student learning through pedagogy or instruction, for example, sometimes extend long after student work has been collected, scored, and analyzed. Further, proposed changes in pedagogy or instruction emerging from this delayed response approach are directed toward future students, not primarily toward currently enrolled students. Meanwhile, equally important assessment questions arise: How well are your currently enrolled students progressing toward achieving high-quality exit-level degree- and program-level outcomes? Is your institution equally, if not more, focused on them? Time gaps that typically exist between assessment cycles or other scheduled assessment periods disengage faculty and other contributors to student learning from the challenges students face in those time gaps. Moreover, the student work that is collected in scheduled assessment time periods represents that of students who have made it to those points in time—the survivors. Without leaving a trace, students who have not survived and the challenges and struggles they encountered are no longer relevant. When what is considered "necessary" assessment is conducted at arm's length from our currently enrolled students, they lose out.

Compelling Reasons to Develop a Comprehensive Real-Time Student Assessment Commitment

Why the urgency to develop a comprehensive real-time assessment commitment to our currently enrolled students? Compelling reasons to do so in the 21st-century United States include:

- continuing diversification of our student demographics (representative of our democracy), representing broad ranges of academic preparation and readiness and personal needs;
- persistent gaps in achievement and degree completion rates between historically represented and historically underrepresented students;
- national dependence on an educated citizenry from across our student demographics to ensure our prosperity, long-term growth, and attentiveness to our democratic values; and
- high demands for students with associate and bachelor's degrees to address evolving needs of the workplace and challenges of globalization.

Within these realities are national calls to improve students' time to degree, make postsecondary education more affordable, respond to the academic and personal needs of our diverse student demographics, and assure student competencies for 21st-century needs. At the same time, for-profit and not-for-profit educational providers are increasingly offering students alternative ways to learn and, more recently, methods for credentialing those alternative ways. These providers may also contract with colleges and universities to deliver courses toward components of a degree or program or an entire program. Enabling students to customize when, where, and even how they prefer to learn—such as through self-paced learning modules and other alternatives—appeals to a broad range of students, not just to those whose work schedules compress their time. Students are also designing new pathways to a degree, expanding previous transfer and coregistration practices. Now, enrolled in one institution, a student may also bundle credits from a range of educational providers such as Coursera, transfer credits from one or several institutions, and seek credentialing for prior learning. Expanding the possible list of alternative education providers to include nontraditional and nonaccredited providers is the U.S. Department of Education's Educational Quality through Innovative Partnerships (EQUIP) experiment. Launched in 2015, EQUIP focuses on providing postsecondary students, primarily low-income students, with other options to learn, such as through massive open online courses (MOOCs) and skills boot camps. Under authorization of its experimental sites initiative, which allows for flexibility in testing the disbursement of financial aid, the Department of Education is pilot testing partnerships between postsecondary institutions and these alternative providers as well as identifying who will serve as third-party accreditors for these models (U.S. Department of Education, 2015).

Outcomes-Based Frameworks and Real-Time Student Assessment

Across the various pathways students follow to obtain a degree, colleges and universities now face this looming question: How do we assure our students equitably achieve a quality degree, no matter when and how they enter our institution? Developments in national and disciplinary, field-based, and professional outcomes-based frameworks provide the shared means for institutions and their programs to illustrate what a quality degree looks like for our students. Over the last decade, two major historic grassroots higher education initiatives have forged a national outcomes-based framework. One is Liberal Education and America's Promise (LEAP), led by the Association of American Colleges & Universities (AAC&U). The other is the Degree Qualifications Profile (DQP), supported by the Lumina Foundation. Collaboratively developed with representatives from a range of postsecondary institutions, these initiatives have identified the liberal learning outcomes of an undergraduate degree as well as a shared set of outcomes for all majors that incorporates those liberal learning outcomes. Providing more specific outcomes-based frameworks for students' fields of study, professions, or disciplines has been the work of two other efforts: (a) competency-based education (CBE) programs that have their roots in military and teacher training and (b) Lumina Foundation's support of Tuning, a collaborative process involving faculty; experts in a field, discipline, or profession; employers; and recent graduates that is focused on identifying the knowledge and skills that students in specific disciplines, professions, or fields of study must demonstrate upon degree completion to transition successfully into their careers. Altogether these frameworks are based on four overarching principles:

1. Equity: Students across our demographics and diverse educational pathways should progress equitably toward achieving a high-quality degree.
2. Transparency: External and internal stakeholders, most importantly our students, should know what undergraduate students are expected to learn and demonstrate: student learning outcomes.
3. Quality: Stated performance criteria applied to students' authentic work define the indicators of students' progress toward and achievement of quality.
4. Explicitness: Pathways to a degree must be (a) clear so students can reduce the uncertainty of time to degree and (b) coherently designed so that students see the relevance of their general education and major program learning across their degree pathways.

Transcending a specific institutional type or mission or even students' diverse pathways to a degree, these outcomes-based frameworks now provide institutions the means to monitor continuously students' equitable progress to a high-quality degree—even if a pathway includes credit for prior learning, transfer of credits, or credentialed coursework from an external provider. Learning outcomes, along with criteria and standards of judgment against which to assess students' progress toward and achievement of quality exit-level expectations, now spell out for external and internal stakeholders what students are expected to learn along their pathways to a quality degree. Focusing on how well students demonstrate their knowledge in their authentic work is challenging the validity of grades and credit hours as representations of a student's learning.

Transparency now exists about what quality looks like in all students' work. Real-time student assessment becomes the continuous means to gauge students' progress toward attaining a quality degree. The unit that drives and builds a comprehensive real-time institutional commitment is the course or educational experience. Assessment results from those individual units are shared and posted on a semester-by-semester basis so that constituencies at the institution and program levels

- "see" and remain chronologically aware of students' progress toward achieving quality exit-level learning outcomes, and
- assume a shared responsibility for addressing students' persistent patterns of underperformance, resulting in a continuous commitment to advance all students to degree completion.

Colleges and universities, other educational providers, and credentialing systems can now work within these shared frameworks and assess student work using scoring rubrics that can be applied to students' outputs or performances across different learning contexts and assignments or experiences. For example, students can demonstrate their critical thinking capacities in a project they complete for their major program or in an assignment in their workplace. What matters now is that assessors have a shared language for nationally developed outcomes and a shared set of criteria and standards of judgment to apply to the work students produce along their degree pathway.

Audience for and Outline of This Book

Real-Time Student Assessment: Meeting the Imperative for Improved Time to Degree, Closing the Opportunity Gap, and Assuring Student Competencies for 21st-Century Needs calls for and helps guide institutions' development of a comprehensive, continuous, and internally motivated assessment commitment.

Beginning with why it is now important to develop a comprehensive real-time student assessment commitment, this book focuses on the responsibilities and principles that underlie an effective approach to help internal stakeholders build a commitment that works effectively in institutional or system contexts. Campus examples put flesh on the bones of this endeavor, aiding internal stakeholders in understanding how institutions and programs prioritize and carry out this process as a commitment to students, not solely as a response to external drivers. Outcomes-based frameworks and agreed-upon aligned scoring rubrics form the foundation of real-time student assessment. Stretched across that foundation is a canvas of interdependent, core learner-centered commitments that support continuous assessment of students' equitable progress toward degree completion. Every course and educational experience contributes to that shared commitment to students. Thus, semester-by-semester course- and experience-based assessment results are reported, interrogated, and acted upon to improve students' patterns of underperformance as they occur and persist along the trajectory of students' degree pathways.

Because this assessment approach is built on campus inclusiveness, this book addresses major constituencies across an institution or system that will contribute in one or more ways to prioritizing, planning, launching, and taking this collaborative effort to scale, and then sustaining the effort. Those constituencies include institution and system leaders; academic and administrative leaders; full- and part-time faculty; representatives from the network of experts who support educating our students, such as teaching assistants, tutors, and individuals in academic support services and educational technology; professionals in faculty development and on the front line of assessment; staff who offer technical support for maintaining and disseminating assessment results; and student representatives who represent the beneficiaries of this effort. Collaboration, cooperation, and inclusiveness together contribute to the sustainability of this living commitment to our currently enrolled students.

"Chapter 1: Current and Projected Student Demographics: Why Equity Matters Now for Individuals and the Nation" identifies compelling reasons for why colleges and universities must commit to develop comprehensive real-time assessment. These conditions include the rapid and continuing shift in our institutions' demographics, with students presenting different levels of academic preparation, readiness, and needs; persistent achievement and completion gaps between historically represented and underrepresented students; and the dependence of our nation and workforce on an educated citizenry across our demographics. More than ever, our institutions are being asked to prepare measurably more students to receive associate and bachelor's degrees across all categories of race, ethnicity, and social and economic difference.

"Chapter 2: Outcomes-Based Frameworks: Equity, Transparency, Quality, and Explicitness" identifies the catalysts that fueled the development of two grassroots outcomes-based initiatives that together now provide institutions with a national framework to monitor currently enrolled students' equitable progress toward achieving a high-quality degree. They are the AAC&U's LEAP and the Lumina Foundation's DQP. Recognizing that many national and specialized accrediting bodies have developed and periodically revise their outcomes-based frameworks, this chapter identifies two other efforts that are contributing to the expansion of outcomes-based frameworks in undergraduate disciplines, professions, and field-based majors: CBE and DQP/Tuning outcomes-based frameworks. These frameworks, along with aligned scoring rubrics or other agreed-upon metrics, now provide institutions and many programs with a shared set of expectations for student learning and a shared set of criteria and standards of judgment to chart students' progress. Over time, these frameworks also have the potential to ensure coherence across the diverse pathways that students pursue to achieve a degree.

"Chapter 3: The Canvas of Core Learner-Centered Commitments That Stretches Across an Outcomes-Based Framework" identifies five core commitments that contribute to developing clear and coherent degree pathways and simultaneously support real-time student assessment:

> Commitment 1: Shared commitment to close existing achievement and graduation gaps measurably
> Commitment 2: Agreement on the language of outcomes and scoring rubrics to identify patterns of performance and underperformance continuously
> Commitment 3: Coherence across the curriculum, cocurriculum, and other educational experiences
> Commitment 4: Alignment of courses, educational experiences, and assignments with outcomes and standards and criteria of judgment
> Commitment 5: Faculty collaboration with the institution's network of experts

The interdependency of these commitments grounds a shared commitment to students' equitable progress, supports the continuous gauging of students' progress based on semester-by-semester reporting of course- and experience-based assessment results and collaborative interrogation of those results, and charts clear and coherent degree pathways for students.

"Chapter 4: Guiding Principles of Real-Time Student Assessment at the Institution and Program Levels" identifies and elaborates on the six principles that underlie an internally driven and shared commitment to real-time assessment. These principles value the contributions of all experts who contribute to students' learning—faculty, advisers, librarians, and professionals in education technology and student support services, for example. Inclusive and collaborative processes of interrogating assessment results and identifying short- and longer-term practices to help students overcome academic challenges deepen those processes. At both the institution and program levels, the following principles underlie continuously monitoring and addressing students' academic challenges throughout their studies, such as developing the cognitive skills of synthesis and analysis or transferring previous learning into new contexts:

> Principle 1: Internally driven and motivated
> Principle 2: Inclusive of internal stakeholders
> Principle 3: Bolstered by collaboration that harnesses others' expertise and practices
> Principle 4: Anchored in continuous reporting and interrogation of assessment results
> Principle 5: Responsive to students' needs in the present tense
> Principle 6: Valued by the institution

As guides, these principles do not dictate the ways in which institutions or programs integrate real-time student assessment into institutional cultures. Four case studies in this chapter illustrate the various ways in which institutions and programs have integrated the six principles. However, closely monitoring students' patterns of performance, interrogating patterns of underperformance, and taking actions to improve those patterns in the present tense are central processes in all the case studies. All focus on supporting currently enrolled students' success. The table at the end of this chapter makes the case for the twenty-first-century relevance of real-time assessment. It compares real-time assessment with more common assessment approaches that occur over longer time intervals. These approaches fall short in directly benefiting those who matter right now: currently enrolled students.

"Chapter 5: Technology That Contributes to Real-Time Student Assessment" identifies some of the major ways that developments or refinements in technology are contributing to the dexterity educators need to move with immediacy from evidence of student learning to actions to improve student learning. This chapter provides an overview of five types of technology that identify heretofore invisible obstacles that students face as they learn, increase access to and allow the interrogation of assessment results, or provide complementary data about student behaviors that enable an institution and its programs to change current practices and policies that inhibit students' persistence to degree. Those five types of technology that contribute to real-time student assessment are:

1. learning management systems (LMSs) or other platforms that collect, synthesize, sort, and report real-time assessment results;
2. assessment management systems (AMSs) that also perform those tasks for an entire institution and its programs;
3. adaptive learning platforms that individualize instruction by addressing learner challenges and reporting on each student's progress and final performance;
4. web-based educational data-mining tools that provide new insights into institution-, program-, and student-level variables that affect students' progress or are predictive of their continued success; and
5. ePortfolios that provide a shared means for faculty, other contributors to student learning, and students themselves to gauge continuously students' equitable progress toward attaining high-quality institution- and program-level outcomes.

Integration of these stand-alone technologies is rapidly occurring across higher education, providing multiple sources of real-time data about student performance. For example, some LMSs already have the capacity to identify students who are at risk of underperforming in their courses based on previous course performance. Increasing access to and on-time analysis of assessment results, these systems collect assessment results, aggregate and disaggregate them, and represent them in a range of visual formats suitable for different stakeholders' analyses. These systems also maintain up-to-date assessment frameworks such as the LEAP outcomes and aligned scoring rubrics that facilitate online scoring.

"Chapter 6: Approaches to Taking Real-Time Student Assessment to Scale" recognizes that real-time student assessment can unsettle some readers because it challenges an institution's or its programs' current assessment mind-set or established practices that satisfy external stakeholders' needs. Reframing, even shifting, what already exists disrupts comfort levels. For that reason, this chapter first identifies some initial approaches that institutions or programs might take—especially at institutions with large enrollments. A narrowed approach to real-time assessment can pave the way toward taking it to scale. Narrowed approaches might gauge students' progress toward achieving quality-level outcomes in all high-risk courses or toward attaining increasingly higher performance levels in outcomes that remain difficult for students to attain, such as critical thinking. Another narrowed approach might focus on continuously tracking the most vulnerable cohorts of students based on early baseline data about them. Four case studies in this chapter illustrate different approaches institutions are taking, such as launching large-scale pilot projects to take to scale their institution's commitment to real-time assessment.

In this book I propose an alternative to more commonly used assessment approaches or mind-sets. It challenges institutions and programs to reform current assessment approaches that are not grounded in continuous real-time evidence of student learning. Proposing change is not without risk: some readers may dismiss real-time student assessment outright as too demanding, time consuming, difficult, or even unnecessary, and remain satisfied with the more familiar and comfortable patterns of their current assessment commitment. Others will perceive the positive potential of change and recognize the urgency of real-time assessment, understanding that this approach is necessary to (a) improve continuously currently enrolled students' learning and (b) enable all students to achieve the outcomes they need for personal fulfillment and to contribute to society.

Institution and program leaders who are open to real-time student assessment may need an effective starting point from which to determine how to initiate this shared commitment to currently enrolled students' success. Evaluating the institution's or its programs' current assessment commitment is that effective starting point. Some institutions, for example, may see the need to reframe the purpose of assessment as a shared commitment to students' success and choose to take some initial steps toward real-time assessment to pilot test this commitment (identified in chapter 6). Others may decide to recalibrate current assessment practices by closing time gaps that currently exist between assessment cycles to gauge currently enrolled students' progress. Still others may learn from colleagues in specialized or nationally accredited programs who have a history of closely monitoring their students' progress and continuously addressing their patterns of underperformance. Campus practices may already exist that are worth emulating or adapting.

The longer an institution takes to develop a shared commitment to real-time student assessment, the less that institution will be able to close opportunity gaps that exist for historically underserved students, keep students on track to degree completion, and ensure students' equitable progress toward quality achievement of the necessary learning outcomes. Time is not on higher education's side.

As a note to readers, for the purposes of this book, *outcomes* and *outcomes-based frameworks* refer broadly to shared expectations for student learning that can be assessed by agreed-upon rubrics or other metrics for the purpose of consistent and continuous assessment of students' authentic work. However, it is important to point out that frameworks vary in how they identify and state those expectations. For example, some frameworks identify "proficiencies" or "competencies." What is nationally significant for higher education is that frameworks exist, providing shared means to assess continuously currently enrolled students' achievement levels.

CURRENT AND PROJECTED STUDENT DEMOGRAPHICS

Why Equity Matters Now for Individuals and the Nation

Broadening access to postsecondary education to students who reflect our national demographics and focusing on all students' persistence toward attaining a high-quality degree have received national attention in this century. A chorus consisting of federal and state officials, policymakers, researchers on student demographics, employers, higher education organizations, and major higher education funders—such as the Bill & Melinda Gates Foundation and the Lumina Foundation—has sustained that attention. Two lead voices in that chorus have been (a) President Barack Obama in his 2009 Address to the Joint Session of Congress, calling for Americans to reach the world's highest rate of college completion by 2020, and (b) the Lumina Foundation, establishing a goal for increasing the proportion of Americans with quality postsecondary degrees, certificates, and other credentials to 60% by 2025 (Lumina Foundation, 2015; White House, 2009). These goals prioritize our nation's pressing need for an educated citizenry that reflects our national demographics—one that contributes to our country's overall societal health and well-being as well as to its economic prosperity in a rapidly changing and globally interconnected world. Within this context, this first chapter makes the following two-part case for why our colleges and universities need to develop a real-time student assessment commitment that continuously improves and, thus, equitably advances all currently enrolled students to achieve a high-quality degree:

- disparities in achievement levels, persistence rates, and graduation rates across our student demographics documented in longitudinally reported national data; and

- national need for more college graduates across our student demographics to contribute to American society at large, to the 21st-century workforce and the demands of globalization, and to students' and their families' social and financial mobility.

Disparities in Achievement Levels, Persistence Rates, and Graduation Rates Across Our Student Demographics: An Overview

Preparing an educated citizenry has been American higher education's historic role, enabling individuals to live fulfilled lives and contribute to the complex and changing civic, social, and economic needs of our nation. Higher percentages of our college-going students reflect and are projected to reflect the diversity of our national demographics. Writing in 2010 about demographic, social, and economic trends in the United States and internationally, Joel Kotkin projected how some of our nation's population percentages will shift by 2050:

> Whites will no longer be the majority. The minority population, currently 30 percent, is expected to exceed 50 percent before 2050. No other advanced populous country will see such diversity.
>
> In fact, most of America's net population growth will be among its minorities, as well as in a growing mixed-race population. Latino and Asian populations are expected to nearly triple, and the children of immigrants will become more prominent. Today in the United States, 25 percent of children under age 5 are Hispanic; by 2050, that percentage will be almost 40 percent. (p. 2)

Our higher education student demographics increasingly reflect this population shift. At the same time, many students across this diverse population face personal and academic challenges. These kinds of obstacles may, for example, impede historically underrepresented students' abilities to persist and achieve a postsecondary degree, contributing to gaps in degree attainment compared with their White and Asian counterparts. Yet, graduating measurably larger percentages of historically underrepresented students remains our current challenge. They represent our immediate and future educated citizenry, the voices of our democracy, and a major source of our workforce. Demographic descriptors provide lenses through which to develop a more granular and dimensional view of who our growing student populations are. In addition to students' race and ethnicity, other major descriptors include students' generation status, nativity (origin of birth), socioeconomic status, and age.

Race and Ethnicity

The National Center for Education Statistics (NCES) identifies the span from 1980 to 2008 as the period during which the racial/ethnic composition of our student bodies shifted. According to its 2010 report,

> Between 1998 and 2008, the racial/ethnic composition of the United States shifted—the White population declined from 80 percent of the total population to 66 percent; the Hispanic population increased from 6 percent of the total to 15 percent; the Black population remained at about 12 percent; and the Asian/Pacific Islander population increased from less than 2 percent of the total population to 4 percent. In 2008, American Indians/Alaska Natives made up about 1 percent and people of two or more races made up about 1 percent of the population. (p. iii)

Based on NCES's actual and projected number of student enrollments in colleges and universities from fall 1996 through fall 2027, based on race/ethnicity, Hussar and Bailey (2011) project the highest percentage of enrollment growth in Black and Hispanic students over the years 2011 to 2022:

- 7 percent increase in enrollment for White students,
- 7 percent for students who are Asian/Pacific Islander,
- 26 percent increase for students who are Black,
- 27 percent increase for students who are Hispanic, and
- stable enrollment of American Indian/Alaska Native. (p. 3)

Longer-term perspectives on continuing diversification are substantiated by demographic data that chart the actual and projected race/ethnicity of high school students. The Western Interstate Commission for Higher Education (WICHE) has been producing high school population forecasts for over 30 years. In its publication *Knocking at the College Door: Projections of High School Graduates,* Prescott and Bransberger (2012) forecast the growth of minority high school students through the 2024–2025 academic year, based on preceding years' documented numbers. In particular, Hispanic students will continue to represent the largest proportion of minority students, followed by Black, Asian, Pacific Islander, and American Indian/Alaska Native students. Table 1.1 illustrates the projected racial/ethnic high school enrollments from 2016 and 2017 through 2024 and 2025.

TABLE 1.1

U.S. Public High School Enrollment (Grades 9–12) by Race/Ethnicity

Academic Year	American Indian/ Alaska Native	Asian/ Pacific Islander	Black, Non-Hispanic	Hispanic	White, Non-Hispanic
2016–2017	181,220	906,630	2,342,617	3,651,757	7,883,751
2017–2018	182,266	944,016	2,320,678	3,752,434	7,840,129
2018–2019	183,841	974,058	2,290,146	3,843,745	7,784,370
2019–2020	188,725	1,006,005	2,286,569	3,966,914	7,696,206
2020–2021	195,390	1,042,209	2,332,654	4,130,834	7,669,705
2021–2022	202,291	1,081,178	2,391,294	4,280,551	7,641,403
2022–2023	207,804	1,110,829	2,442,290	4,371,350	7,582,449
2023–2024	208,826	1,133,428	2,459,086	4,362,706	7,517,304
2024–2025	205,657	1,140,483	2,426,542	4,248,975	7,389,783

Source. Prescott & Bransberger, 2012, p. 32. Used with permission from WICHE.

Based on their high school projections, Prescott and Bransberger (2013) conclude that the public graduating high school classes are "inching ever closer to becoming 'majority-minority,' in which no single race/ethnicity accounts for 50 percent of the total" (pp. 1–2).

Of national importance are longitudinal data that report persistent six-year graduation gaps between White and Asian students and their Black, Hispanic, Pacific Islander, and American Indian/Alaska Native counterparts. These data are based on first-time, full-time student enrollments, generally representing traditional-age students. An NCES (2013) report on increased numbers of students entering four-year institutions across racial/ethnic lines in 2005 (the first year that a percentage for Pacific Islander students was reported by NCES) and graduating six years later concluded that

> Asian students again showed the highest six-year graduation rates, followed by White student graduation rates.
>
> - 69 percent of Asian students
> - 62 percent of White students
> - 51 percent of Hispanic students
> - 49 percent of Pacific Islander students
> - 40 percent of Black students
> - 40 percent of American Indian/Alaska Native students

Six-year graduation rates for students entering four-year institutions two years later in 2007 remain similar to those for students who entered in 2005 (NCES, 2015).

Two recent Education Trust reports, issued in 2015 and 2016, focus on the good news and not-so-good news about underrepresented students' graduation rates at public four-year institutions, the sector that enrolls more than two-thirds of undergraduate students. Eberle-Sudre, Welch, and Nichols (2015) analyzed graduation rates at 255 public institutions that reported overall graduation rate increases in graduation cohorts that had at least 50 minority and 50 White students in them over the 2003–2013 period. Although graduation rates increased for minorities at these institutions, "the completion gap narrowed by slightly more than half a percentage point (0.6), leaving a 14-point completion gap" (p. 2). More recently, Nichols, Eberle-Sudre, and Welch (2016) examined graduation rates across specific underrepresented groups during that same 10-year span. They concluded that at four-year public institutions across the country, "graduation rates for Black students have not improved as much as those of White students" (p. 1). Targeting 232 public four-year institutions that reported increases in graduation rates, these authors found that Latino and Native students actually made more progress toward graduation than their White peers, whereas Black students "made less progress" (p. 1).

Disparities also exist between male and female students across all racial/ethnic groups. According to NCES's *Higher Education: Gaps in Access and Persistence Study* (2012), persistence and graduation rate disparities exist between the educational attainment of male and female students. Among first-time students seeking bachelor's degrees who started full-time at a four-year college in 2004, a higher percentage of females than males completed those degrees within six years (61% versus 56%). This pattern held across all racial/ethnic groups, although the gap was widest between Black females and males (9 percentage points; p. xv).

The fastest-growing minority populations documented in Table 1.1 are also those representing lower college graduation rates than those of White and Asian students. Describing those populations among recent high school graduates, Prescott and Bransberger (2013) conclude that these students "are less well prepared academically and have far fewer financial resources at their disposal, on average" (p. 7). Thus, we can expect that high percentages of high school students will continue to require developmental coursework. Yet placement into developmental coursework itself is directly related to low retention and graduation patterns. In 2011, NCES reported that approximately 1.7 million students begin college remediation each year. Of those students, only one in 10 reach graduation (p. 342). According to Complete College America (2012) in *Remediation: Higher Education's Bridge to Nowhere*, "More than 50 percent of students entering two-year colleges and nearly 20 percent of those entering four-year universities are placed in remedial classes." Experiencing frustration upon learning about this placement, "thousands who were accepted into college never show up for classes" (p. 2).

Generation Status and Nativity

Generation status and nativity, excluding nonresidential foreign students who account currently for about 20% of our college enrollment (Institute of International Education, 2014) are closely related factors that have bearing on students' educational attainment. From 1970 to 2007, Staklis and Horn (2012) report, the U.S. foreign-born population tripled to more than 37 million, or one in eight U.S. residents (p. 1). The authors also identify that the fastest-growing immigrant populations in the country as of 2010 are from Mexico (29.4%) and Southeast Asia (24.9%) (2012, Table 4).

Those who are the first in their family to go to college are represented in the racial/ethnic diversity of our full- and part-time student populations. These students include (a) first-generation American-born students whose parent or parents do not hold a postsecondary degree, and (b) first- and second-generation immigrant students, also coming from households in which a parent or parents do not hold a degree. According to Nicole Smith (2013) of the Georgetown University McCourt School of Public Policy, approximately one-third of undergraduates are first-generation students and "disproportionately African American and Hispanic" (slides 2–5). Approximately one-third of first-generation students attending college are over 30 years old. They "tend to work longer hours at their jobs, are less likely to live on campus, and are more likely to have parents who would struggle to complete financial-aid forms" (Smith, 2013, slides 2–5). In addition, three out of five of these students do not complete a degree within six years (Smith, 2013). They are more likely than non-first-generation students to arrive academically unprepared, requiring remediation before they can take courses for credit (Tym, McMillion, Barone, Webster, 2004, pp. 1, 8).

Similar to U.S. children, children of college-educated immigrants are more likely to succeed in college than children of immigrant parents who did not receive a postsecondary education. Also, similar to U.S. children from poor families, those who come from poor immigrant families typically struggle academically as well. Country of origin, family income, and family education account for different success rates across first-generation immigrant students. For example, according to Baum and Flores (2011), students from China, Japan, and many African countries have high success rates, whereas those from "Mexico, Guatemala, Haiti, Laos and Cambodia fare less well" (p. 186). Across the Hispanic population, children born in the United States have higher postsecondary attainment rates than those born outside of the United States (Baum & Flores, 2011, p. 42).

Socioeconomic Status

Students' socioeconomic backgrounds, identified by family income, represent another demographic factor in degree attainment. Historically, students from poor families have been disproportionately represented in our colleges and universities compared with students from higher-income households. According to the American Council on Education's (ACE) 2015 analysis of U.S. Census data in the years since 2008, there has actually been a drop in the percentage of low-income students who immediately enroll in colleges and universities after high school graduation. The study reports a decline "by 10 percentage points since 2008, from 56 percent of graduates to just 46 percent" (Nellum & Hartle, 2015). This significant drop occurs as graduation rates have been rising. Based on the 2012 data, the most recent year for which NCES data were available on college enrollments, Desilver (2014) affirms that pattern. The percentage of low-income high school completers attending college (including graduates as well as people who completed an equivalency degree and who are age 16 to 24) continues to trail that of higher-income students (Desilver, 2014). The 2015 ACE study identifies reasons that may account for low-income students' lower postsecondary enrollments: they view the cost of postsecondary education as out of reach for them, they need to become immediately employed after high school, and they do not see the value of a college degree (Nellum & Hartle, 2015).

Income also affects degree attainment. According to Baum, Ma, and Payea (2013), the percentage of students from the highest family income quintile earning bachelor's degrees within six years is "twice as high as the percentage of students from the lowest family income quintile" (p. 33). Contributing to lower college graduation rates for low-income students is a confluence of factors, including limited access to quality education along students' entire primary and secondary education, lack of knowledge about what courses to take to prepare for college-level work, and lack of guidance about the kinds of colleges or universities that would best match them (White House, 2014, pp. 13–22). Low-income students' access to and attainment of a postsecondary degree became a focus of the Obama administration in 2014 when the president called for increasing this cohort's participation in higher education as a means to advance the percentage of Americans who hold a postsecondary degree or certificate (Field, 2014).

Age

Another demographic descriptor that contributes to our understanding of persistence and graduation rates is age. The largest-growing segment of our college-going population consists of non-traditional-age students (age 25 or older) representing all races, ethnicities, socioeconomic groups, and different generations and countries of origin. Reporting on enrollment patterns for traditional and non-traditional-age students, in 2005 NCES projected enrollments for those groups to 2023. The rate of increase for students under age 25 will be 12%, compared with the rate of 20% for students age 25 and over (NCES, 2005). The cumulative effect for this growing population is that these students are "quickly becoming as traditional a part of the college-going population as younger students are" (Prescott & Bransberger, 2012, p. vii).

The non-traditional-age population carries with it a vast set of attributes that further underscore students' personal challenges. The 2012 Advisory Committee on Student Financial Assistance report to Congress and the Secretary of Education identified non-traditional-age students as the "largest subset of students in the nation," one that is "virtually impossible to define or label" (p. iii), given this population's demographic and socioeconomic characteristics. To illustrate the breadth of subgroups subsumed under this student demographic, the report identifies 27 characteristics, among which are the following: working poor, unemployed, first-generation, historically underrepresented minorities, students with dependent children, veterans, homeless, and public assistance recipients (Advisory Committee on Student Financial Assistance, 2012, p. 89). Now included in the non-traditional-age student population are the 31 million students who went to college in the last 20 years but have dropped out—a finding reported in the National Student Clearinghouse Research Center's (2014), *Some College, No Degree: A National View of Students With Some College Enrollment but No Completion*. Of that total population, one-third enrolled at a single institution for a single term. The remaining students who completed at least two terms of enrollment, referred to as "multiple-term enrollees," represent yet another non-traditional-age subgroup that still has the potential to complete a degree (pp. 2–3).

Senior citizens are now extending the age range of this college-going group. Citing U.S. Census data, director of the Higher Education Initiative for Encore.org and former president of Goddard College, Barbara Vacarr (2014) reports that by 2030 the population of people over 55 will be 112 million—an increase of 76 million from today. She views this group as a new student market, given senior citizens' life expectancy and desire to develop a new chapter in their lives. She writes, "4.5 million

Americans age 50–70—6 percent of the population—are in active second careers today, engaging in purposeful work that contributes to the greater good."

Lower persistence and graduation rate patterns exist across non-traditional-age students, "who are more likely to enroll part-time in college and less likely to persist and complete degree programs than full-time traditional students" (Advisory Committee on Student Financial Assistance, 2012, p. 1). Complicating their educational commitment are the layers of work, financial, and family commitments that challenge their chronological persistence to completing a degree. Age also has bearing on nontraditional students' completion rates, according to the National Student Clearinghouse Research Center (2012). A degree completion gap exists between younger and older non-traditional-age students, the "latter group having a much lower six-year completion rate, 57 percent vs. 42 percent" (National Student Clearinghouse Research Center, 2012, p. 2).

Many students across higher education's demographic diversity have narrower academic preparation than traditional-age, White, Asian, non-first-generation, and higher-income-family students. Those lower levels of academic preparation, stemming from the sets of circumstances described previously have short- and longer-term consequences. Weak academic preparation thwarts early college success and even longer-term success, leading to students' decisions to drop out. Individual cultural, familial, financial, and employment factors or combinations of these factors also affect students' ability to sustain their undergraduate studies. Thus, for example, included in the Hispanic and Black student population are not only first-generation U.S.-born students but also first-generation students from immigrant families. Immigrant parents often do not speak English, lack understanding of how to support their children academically, and rely on the financial contributions of their college-going children to support the family. Included in all races and ethnicities are students from very low to very high socioeconomic groups, reflecting different levels of academic preparation, readiness, and self-direction. Included in all races and ethnicities are non-traditional-age students who face challenges such as working full-time, rearing a family, and maybe taking care of their parents as well. Yet, even when the odds seem to be against students, many overcome them. Hoxby and Avery's (2013) study on high-achieving, low-income students illustrates that not all low-income students are low achievers, and Harper and associates' (2014) interviews with college-bound New York City Black and Latino males remain important testaments to individuals' potential and commitment to succeed—even in the face of academic or personal circumstances that challenge their success. Remaining aware of the range of our students' needs and challenges provides reason enough to gauge closely all students' progress toward achieving a high-quality degree—a matter of equity.

The Nation's Need for More Students With Postsecondary Degrees

Describing universities as "agents of social mobility" and "distributors of life chances," Little and Arthur (2010, p. 293) contribute to making the case for why focusing on our currently enrolled students' equitable progress toward attaining a high-quality degree matters. In particular, achieving an undergraduate degree grounded in study of the liberal arts and students' chosen major, profession, or field of study provides students with the knowledge, skills, and lifelong capacities that benefit their personal development. In the words of Baum and colleagues (2013), that postsecondary degree changes "the way people approach their lives" (p. 10). In addition, higher educational attainment increases individuals' opportunities for social and economic mobility compared with those individuals who do not attain a postsecondary degree. Moreover, the value of a postsecondary degree extends to other beneficiaries by increasing the likelihood of degreed students' social and civic engagement. Specifically, society at large benefits. The workforce itself benefits from students whose undergraduate degrees prepare them to contribute to the nation's current and future economic development.

The Value of a Postsecondary Degree That Extends From the Individual to Society

Presenting detailed chronological documentation supporting the value of an undergraduate degree, Baum and colleagues (2013) identify the multiple ways in which individuals and society both benefit from students who attain an associate or a bachelor's degree compared with individuals who do not. Attaining a degree increases the likelihood that students will

- earn more in their lifetime,
- advance their income,
- enjoy better working conditions,
- move up the socioeconomic ladder,
- lead healthier lifestyles,
- become more active citizens, and
- increase the prospects that the "next generation" will prosper.

Compared with individuals who do not attain an undergraduate degree, people with degrees typically have increased opportunities for employment and future financial gain. Findings from a recent Pew Research Center (2014) survey of 2,002 adults reflect the widening income gap between those with a high school diploma and those with a college degree. According to the survey, "The median annual earnings for full-time working college-degree holders, millennials, ages 25 to 32, are $17,500 greater than for those with high school diplomas" (p. 3). In addition, an undergraduate degree affords college graduates other personal advantages, such as improved health, quality of life, and job satisfaction (Buckles, Hagemann, Malamud, Morrill, & Wozniak, 2013; Faber, n.d.). Of equal importance to individuals is the value of the liberal education component of students' undergraduate degree, a value best articulated in the work of two national higher education organizations: the Association of American Colleges & Universities (AAC&U) and the Council of Independent Colleges (CIC). Both organizations focus on the importance of students' engagement in ideas, disciplinary and interdisciplinary perspectives, and ways of knowing that expand individuals' approaches to problemsolving and drive their intellectual curiosity.

Beneficiaries extend beyond the individuals who hold a postsecondary degree. Boyer (1990) spoke to the societal aim of higher education. It not only prepares students for productive careers but also enables them

> to live lives of dignity and purpose; not only to generate new knowledge, but to channel that knowledge to humane ends; not merely to study government, but to help shape a citizenry that can promote the public good. (p. 160)

Higher levels of education translate into the likelihood of students' social and civic engagement (Davila & Mora, 2007; Verba, Schlozman, & Brady, 1995). Students with postsecondary degrees volunteer, serve on local boards to address community needs, or advocate in even wider social or political contexts for civil rights and equitable application of the principles of our democracy. These kinds of social and civic commitments realize the potential of higher education to "fuel an engaged and healthy citizenry and a civil society (a role that is equally important, if less easily measured)" (Prescott & Bransberger, 2012, p. xi).

Attaining a degree, particularly for individuals from historically underrepresented populations and those who are the first of their generation to attend college, also increases the possibility that those graduates' children will follow their parents' educational path. In turn, that next generation will also benefit personally and economically from an undergraduate education as well as contribute to strengthening the social fabric of our nation to mirror our national demographics.

The Larger Economic Value of a Postsecondary Degree

Employers today are placing a premium on hiring students who hold post-secondary degrees or credentials. President Obama targeted the national importance of educating Americans across our national demographics to meet workplace demands: "Earning a postsecondary degree or credential is no longer just a pathway to opportunity for a talented few; rather, it is a prerequisite for the growing jobs of the new economy" (White House, n.d.). Within the national and global context of the "new economy," Prescott and Bransberger (2013) focus on higher education's role in educating all students: "More than ever, our national prosperity and security, in a globalized labor market driven by the prevalence of well-educated, highly skilled workers, depend on improving our performance with underrepresented populations" (p. 7).

Employers rely on our colleges and universities to prepare students not only for careers but also with what AAC&U (2005) identifies in *Liberal Education and America's Promise* as the "intellectual and practical skills" that define the outcomes of students' liberal education, such as critical thinking, creatively, writing, speaking, teamwork, intercultural knowledge, and competence. (See also pp. 31–32 in chapter 2.) In fact, high percentages of employers prioritize these skills over students' chosen field proficiencies when they make a hiring choice, documented in periodic employer surveys commissioned by AAC&U beginning in 2006. In a 2013 survey by Hart Research Associates, 9 out of 10 employers said it was important that they hire students who demonstrate "ethical judgment and integrity; intercultural skills; and the capacity for continued new learning." Ninety-five percent of the employers surveyed agree that candidates' capacities "to think critically, communicate clearly, and solve complex problems are more important than their undergraduate major." Ninety-five percent said they give hiring preference to college graduates with the "intellectual and interpersonal skills that will help them to contribute to innovation in the workplace" (Hart Research Associates, "Overview," 2013, p. 1; see also pp. 31–32 in chapter 2 on employers' endorsement of AAC&U's Essential Learning Outcomes).

Based on a federal database analyzing qualifications of 1,100 different jobs, researcher and economist Anthony Carnevale reports there is "consistent evidence that the highest salaries apply to positions that call for intensive use of liberal education capacities" (Humphreys & Carnevale, 2016, slide 43). Among the capacities Carnevale identifies are "writing, inductive and deductive reasoning, judgment and decision making, problem-solving skills, social/interpersonal skills, mathematics, and originality" (slide 43). Bransberger and Prescott (2012) also identify high-level skills and innovation as essential to meet the competitive labor market in our economy's global context, "where educational attainment is a profoundly important signal of the capabilities of both individuals and societies" (p. xii). In *Dancing With Robots: Human Skills for Computerized Work*, Levy and Murnane (2013) target three kinds of work that will be increasingly valued in this century's workforce: "solving unstructured problems, working with new information, and carrying out non-routine manual tasks" (p. 3). The authors focus on the multiple ways in which computerization and technology, including robotics, are rapidly replacing humans performing routine or replicable tasks. As technology takes over those kinds of tasks, employers need to hire individuals who demonstrate higher-order thinking skills, such as the ability to solve muddy, unscripted problems—ones that computers are currently unable to solve.

> The human mind's strength is its flexibility—the ability to process and integrate many kinds of information to perform a complex task. The computer's strengths are speed and accuracy, not flexibility, and computers are best at performing tasks for which logical rules or a statistical model lay out a path to a solution. (Levy & Murnane, 2013, p. 9)

National pressure to prepare more students across our student demographics with associate and bachelor's degrees is at an all-time high. This pressure adds to why it matters that our institutions monitor closely our currently enrolled students' equitable progress toward degree completion and address students' academic challenges as they arise. However, at our current graduation rates, according to Carnevale, Smith, and Strohl, our institutions will not meet projected employment needs. In their 2010 summary of hiring projections through 2018, *Help Wanted: Projections of Jobs and Education Requirements Through 2018*, the authors warned that our nation is on a "collision course with the future" (p. 4) because not enough Americans are attaining a degree. And that degree is what employers will increasingly seek, leaving behind high school graduates and dropouts. Citing abundant employment statistics from the Georgetown University Center on Education and the Workforce, in 2014 the authors updated their workforce projections to 2020 in *Recovery: Job Growth and Education Requirements Through 2020*. In this update, Carnevale and colleagues projected that by 2020 an "estimated 65 percent of jobs in the economy will require some form of postsecondary education and training," and that "the United States will fall short by 5 million workers with postsecondary education—at the current production rate" (p. 2).

The Lumina Foundation's tracking of the percentage of working adults who hold postsecondary degrees and credentials also focuses on the national importance of preparing more degreed students across our student demographics. According to the most recent available data in 2014, 45.3% of working adults, ages 25 to 64, hold an associate or bachelor's degree—a percentage that inched upward from 37.9% in 2008 to 40.0% in 2013 (Lumina Foundation, 2016b). Reflecting the disparities in graduation rates identified in this chapter are the percentages of working-age adults (25–64 years old) who hold either an associate or a bachelor's degree based on population groups reported in the 2012–2014 U.S. Census Bureau American Community Survey One-Year PUMS files, shown in Table 1.2.

TABLE 1.2

Degree-Attainment Rates Among U.S. Residents (Ages 25–64), by Population Group

Population Group	Percentage (%)
Asian	60.6
White	45.1
Black	28.7
Native American	23.7
Hispanic	20.9

Source. Lumina Foundation, 2016b. From U.S. Census Bureau, 2012, 2013, and 2014 American Community Survey One-Year PUMS files.

Yet another perspective on our country's graduation rates comes from the Organisation for Economic Co-operation and Development (OECD), which reports on performance of education systems across 34 member countries and a number of partner countries. Percentage of four-year college graduation rates of students ages 25 to 64 is one indicator used to rank countries' educational performance. Reporting on that indicator for 2012, the OECD (2014) ranked U.S. graduation rates 19th out of the 28 countries reporting at that time (Chart A1.1–A1.1a). In contrast, in "1995 the United States ranked second after New Zealand based on the higher education graduation rates of 19 reporting OECD countries" (OECD, 2012, p. 2 & Chart A1.1).

Addressing those who argue that not everyone needs or should strive to achieve a college education, Prescott and Bransberger (2013) argue as follows:

But the overwhelming evidence tells us that higher levels of educational attainment are essential, now and in the future, if our country is to compete in an increasingly globalized economy and if individuals are to compete for jobs that provide a living wage—jobs that increasingly demand an education beyond high school.

Assuring that students across our demographics equitably achieve a high-quality postsecondary degree is nationally important, advancing not only an individual and his or her family's future but also society at large and our evolving workplace needs that emerge from our national and global context and ever-changing developments in technology that shape how people work, communicate, discover, plan and make decisions. (p. vii)

Prioritizing this goal would have the following effects, among others:

- advancing individuals and their families, increasing the likelihood of their social and economic mobility;
- addressing the needs of our democratic society at large, such as by reducing inequities across our diverse populations; and
- facing the evolving needs of our workforce, which relies not only on students' disciplinary or professional knowledge and skills but also on the intellectual and practical skills developed in general education and further honed in students' major programs of study.

Unless we pay close attention to our currently enrolled students' equitable academic progress toward attaining a high-quality degree, we will not live up to one of our nation's founding principles: equality. In *Thirteen Economic Facts About Social Mobility and the Role of Education*, authors Greenstone, Looney, Patashnik, and Yu (2013) project the long-term negative consequences of our uneven graduation rates: "Rising disparities in college completion portend rising disparities in outcomes in the future" (p. 11).

2

OUTCOMES-BASED
FRAMEWORKS

Equity, Transparency, Quality, and Explicitness

Two historic grassroots initiatives in higher education, the Association of American Colleges & Universities' (AAC&U's) Liberal Education and America's Promise (LEAP) and the Lumina Foundation's Degree Qualifications Profile (DQP), now provide postsecondary institutions with a national outcomes-based framework. This framework identifies what all graduates should know and be able to do based on the two major components of a student's degree: a liberal education and a major program of study. Additionally, two other major initiatives in this century are expanding the development of outcomes-based frameworks in disciplines, professions, and fields of study: the Lumina Foundation's DQP/Tuning and the federal government's 2013 authorization to approve new models for delivering competency-based education (CBE) programs and degrees.

What fueled the development of these frameworks? Equity, transparency, quality, and explicitness. Persistent disparities in achievement and degree completion rates between historically represented and underrepresented students, coupled with the nation's need for more degreed students across our student demographics, brought into focus institutions' need to develop a sustained commitment to monitor all students' progress—a commitment to equity. Lack of clarity among internal and external stakeholders, including students, about what undergraduates specifically learn as a result of the liberal education and major program components of a degree brought into focus the importance of stating expectations for student learning—a commitment to transparency represented in student learning outcomes. Lack of clarity with those same audiences about what quality looks like in our undergraduate students' work also brought into focus the need to develop publicly shared performance criteria—scoring rubrics—that describe quality expectations for all students. Students' uncertainty about time to degree brought into focus the need for institutions to reform long-standing academic policies, practices, or protocols to streamline degree pathways—explicitness. For example, traditional academic-year scheduling of day and evening courses did not accommodate non-traditional-age working students' schedules, a hurdle that thwarted students' abilities to stay on track to a degree or even to persist. Students required to take and pass a sequence of non-credit-bearing developmental courses before they were allowed to take credit-bearing courses have faced the same uncertainty about their time to degree. Development of clear and coherent pathways helps students gauge their progress toward a degree as well as see the relevance of their coursework, including previously credentialed work.

In the first two parts of this chapter, I describe the two grassroots outcomes-based initiatives that together now provide institutions with a shared framework to monitor currently enrolled students' equitable progress toward achieving a high-quality degree: AAC&U's LEAP and the Lumina Foundation's DQP. Recognizing that many national and specialized accrediting bodies, such as in nursing, have already established professional or disciplinary outcomes-based frameworks, the next part of the chapter describes two recent initiatives in students' fields of study, disciplines, or professions that promote the expansion of outcomes-based frameworks across postsecondary education: DQP/Tuning and new models of CBE. Finally, I discuss the wider potential of outcomes-based frameworks to provide coherence along students' diverse pathways to a degree.

LEAP: Essential Learning Outcomes and Aligned Scoring Rubrics

At the turn of this century the AAC&U focused on the role of our institutions' liberal education within the contexts of higher education's shifting demographics, growing economic and social inequities between those who are educated and those who are not, and the escalating educational needs of our society and workplace. In 2002 the AAC&U published *Greater Expectations: A New Vision for Learning as a Nation Goes to College,* its landmark call for and vision of a "dramatic reorganization of undergraduate education to ensure that all college aspirants receive not just access to college, but an education of lasting value" (p. vii). That vision identifies what undergraduates across all majors should be learning in this century, how they should learn, and how we would know that they are learning. Equity, transparency, quality, and explicitness are central to that vision. It is specifically built on "the belief that all students are capable of high level learning" and a "commitment to inclusiveness and equal access to high quality college education for all individuals and groups" (AAC&U, 2002, p. 46). Among other shared commitments, *Greater Expectations* specifies the importance of

- clear and coherent expectations of achievement, aligned throughout educational levels (eventually K–12 as well);
- focus on learning and the quality of student accomplishment;
- concerted action by all stakeholders; and
- a culture of evidence based on assessment and accountability. (p. 46)

The AAC&U's *Greater Expectations* also identifies a corresponding set of institutional action steps that enable campuses to achieve the landmark vision. These steps focus on an institution's educational system, curricular design, faculty roles and responsibilities, and classroom practices that chronologically engage all students across higher education's demographics and position them to apply their liberal learning outcomes in increasingly more complex contexts, including real-life unscripted problems (AAC&U, 2002, pp. 47–53).

A national public advocacy and campus action initiative to advance the *Greater Expectations* vision was launched in 2005—LEAP—championing "the importance of a 21st-century liberal education—for individual students and for a nation dependent on economic creativity and democratic vitality" (AAC&U, 2005, p. 1). A major commitment that grew out of the LEAP initiative was the collaborative development of a national outcomes-based framework that defines *quality undergraduate achievement* by identifying a shared set of liberal learning outcomes that all undergraduates should be able to demonstrate. A grassroots commitment involving teams of faculty and other academic and student affairs professionals from over 100 higher education institutions, representing two- and four-year institutions with diverse missions, collated sets of essential general education outcomes collected from institutions across the country. The list of essential learning outcomes (ELOs) is the result of that historic collaborative work. That list calls for students' demonstration of liberal learning outcomes across four categories that extend from an institution's general education or core curriculum program across students' major programs of study. Figure 2.1 identifies those four categories and the ELOs under each category.

Figure 2.1. AAC&U's essential learning outcomes.

The Essential Learning Outcomes

★ ★ ★ ★ ★ ★ ★ ★ ★ ★ ★ ★ ★ ★ ★ ★ ★

Beginning in school, and continuing at successively higher levels across their college studies, students should prepare for 21st-century challenges by gaining:

✴ **Knowledge of Human Cultures and the Physical and Natural World**

- Through study in the sciences and mathematics, social sciences, humanities, histories, languages, and the arts

Focused by engagement with big questions, both contemporary and enduring

✴ **Intellectual and Practical Skills, including**

- Inquiry and analysis
- Critical and creative thinking
- Written and oral communication
- Quantitative literacy
- Information literacy
- Teamwork and problem solving

Practiced extensively, across the curriculum, in the context of progressively more challenging problems, projects, and standards for performance

✴ **Personal and Social Responsibility, including**

- Civic knowledge and engagement—local and global
- Intercultural knowledge and competence
- Ethical reasoning and action
- Foundations and skills for lifelong learning

Anchored through active involvement with diverse communities and real-world challenges

✴ **Integrative and Applied Learning, including**

- Synthesis and advanced accomplishment across general and specialized studies

Demonstrated through the application of knowledge, skills, and responsibilities to new settings and complex problems

 Association of American Colleges & Universities

 LEAP

Note. This listing was developed through a multiyear dialogue with hundreds of colleges and universities about needed goals for student learning; analysis of a long series of recommendations and reports from the business community; and analysis of the accreditation requirements for engineering, business, nursing, and teacher education. The findings are documented in previous publications of the AAC&U's: *College Learning for the New Global Century* (2007) and *The LEAP Vision for Learning* (2011). For more information, see www.aacu.org/leap

Reprinted with the permission of the AAC&U.

The *LEAP Employer-Educator Compact: Making Quality a Priority as Americans Go to College* is a testament both to the national importance of all students being able to demonstrate quality-level achievement of the ELOs and the relevance of those outcomes to our national and workforce demands (AAC&U, 2013; see also chapter 1, p. 24). Agreeing that too many college students "leave college lacking crucial capacities that they—and society— urgently need," leaders of higher education institutions and leaders of organizations and companies that hire undergraduates came together to prioritize "quality of student learning on national, regional, state, and institutional agendas for the benefit of our students, our economy, and our democracy" (AAC&U, 2013, p. 2). Extending the invitation to other leaders to join, signatories of this compact, representing 250 current leaders, identify the four categories of LEAP outcomes represented in Figure 2.1 as the hallmark of 21st-century learning and pledge to focus with "new intensity" on

1. the learning college students most need both for the economy and for democracy;
2. 21st-century designs for high-quality, hands-on learning that prepare students to deal with complexity, diversity, and change; and
3. the development of meaningful evidence about students' actual achievement in college. (AAC&U, 2013, p. 1)

From 2007 to 2009, AAC&U launched a related project to flesh out the ELOs: development of Valid Assessment of Learning in Undergraduate Education (VALUE) scoring rubrics that align with the ELOs (AAC&U, 2014a). As illustrated by representative examples in Appendix 2A and Appendix 2B, these rubrics translate each ELO into corresponding essential attributes and levels of progress—Benchmark 1, Milestone 2, Milestone 3—toward achieving high-quality exit-level achievement: Capstone 4. The ELOs and the VALUE rubrics have both now been mainstreamed into higher education as an equitable means of chronologically assessing students' progress toward achieving high-quality, exit-level, liberal learning outcomes. Faculty and other educational professionals are applying these rubrics or adaptations of them to the broad range of undergraduate work that students produce demonstrating their attainment of liberal learning outcomes at increasingly higher levels. These rubrics were not designed based on a standardized or universal assignment. They were designed to identify the criteria that represent the essential dimensions of each of the ELOs. Students should be able to demonstrate these dimensions in the multiple kinds of authentic work they prepare along their educational pathways, including in their major programs of study and the cocurriculum. Diverse opportunities to practice an institution's set of ELOs, coupled with feedback from educators and peers and students' self-reflection against the aligned rubrics, contribute to students' progress toward achieving an institution's set of ELOs at the capstone level.

The ELOs and VALUE rubrics have moved beyond single-campus use. Two large-scale projects, statewide and multistate, have been piloting the ELOs and VALUE rubrics as a shared means to assess students' liberal learning outcomes and also represent a possible alternative to standardized tests.

Launched in 2010 under Massachusetts's commissioner Richard Freeland, the Advancing a Massachusetts Culture of Assessment (AMCOA) pilot project was designed to develop an agreed-upon means of reporting students' exit-level achievement across the state's 28 public institutions. Specifically, a proposed report would address two goals of a statewide agenda: (a) "achieving higher levels of student learning through better assessment and more extensive use of assessment results," and (b) "closing achievement gaps among students from different ethnic, racial, and income groups in all areas of educational progress" (Massachusetts Department of Higher Education, 2015). Representatives across Massachusetts's 28 public higher education institutions took a firm position against using standardized tests to document student learning in favor of scoring authentic student work that more appropriately and accurately represents what institutions or their programs value. Focusing on three of the ELOs—written communication, critical thinking, and quantitative literacy—and using the aligned VALUE rubrics, representatives from participating institutions practiced scoring samples of upper-level student work from campuses involved in the pilot scoring. This pilot has led to a larger statewide focus on developing assignments that align with ELOs and expanding the number of campuses involved in future scheduled scoring sessions.

Lessons learned from the AMCOA project about identifying, collecting, and scoring student work using the VALUE rubrics informed a large-scale multistate pilot project. With support from the Bill & Melinda Gates Foundation, the Multi-State Collaborative to Advance Learning Outcomes Assessment (MSC)—under the direction of AAC&U and the State Higher Education Executive Officers Association (SHEEO)—was launched in 2011 to pilot test the feasibility of using the VALUE rubrics as cross-institutional means to score and report on student outcomes. This pilot also tested the feasibility of scoring students' authentic work to document undergraduate learning as an alternative to standardized tests. Fifty-three institutions representing both two-year and four-year institutions in nine states (Connecticut, Indiana, Kentucky, Massachusetts, Minnesota, Missouri, Oregon, Rhode Island, and Utah) engaged in a proof-of-concept pilot study focused on applying the critical thinking, written communication, and quantitative literacy VALUE rubrics to samples of student work submitted by those 53 institutions. Specifically, the pilot tested collaboratively developed protocols for

- identifying and collecting students' near-graduation work—an initial attempt to report on students' performance close to the end of their studies;
- developing a methodology to ensure validity and reliability in scoring large samples of student work; and

- developing a web-based platform in Taskstream's assessment management system, Aqua, that enables large numbers of faculty to score student work online asynchronously.

In this pilot the sample consisted of over 7,000 work samples scored by 126 faculty from participating institutions. Faculty went through preparatory interrater reliability scoring sessions and did not score student work from their own institutions.

Results of the proof-of-concept initial pilot were announced in fall 2015. They attest to the feasibility of identifying, collecting, and scoring large samples of student work online. In addition, results of the pilot attest to the capacity of the web-based Aqua system to aggregate and disaggregate scoring results based on how members of the project wanted to view the results. (For examples of ways in which assessment management systems visually represent scoring results, see chapter 5, pp. 123–126). Among the significant findings of this proof-of-concept pilot are the following:

- The VALUE rubrics used in the study encompassed key elements of each learning outcome studied and were very useful for assessing student work and for improving assignments.
- Actionable data about student achievement of key learning outcomes on specific key dimensions of these important learning outcomes can be generated via a common rubric-based assessment approach (AAC&U, 2015a).

The study also found that "faculty can effectively use common rubrics to evaluate student work products—even those produced for courses outside of their areas of expertise." Importantly, that finding dispels the belief that only standardized tests can objectively and reliably evaluate our students' performance levels. Although the results of scoring from this pilot project were not intended to be generalized beyond this sample from nine states, they attest to the effectiveness of faculty scoring. Similar to national test results, faculty scores for critical thinking also identify this outcome as one that college students need to develop: "Of the three outcomes evaluated, far fewer students were achieving at high levels on a variety of dimensions of critical thinking than did so for written communication or quantitative literacy" (AAC&U, 2015a). Scores for critical thinking document lower levels of achievement in the dimensions of students' abilities "to use evidence to investigate a point of view or reach a conclusion" and "to analyze the influence of context and assumptions" (AAC&U, 2015a; Lederman, 2015).

Compared to standardized test scores, the educator-designed VALUE rubrics offer results that have immediate relevance to a campus based on its own student samples viewed through the eyes of peer scorers from other campuses. Context-specific results generate collaborative discussions about ways to improve pedagogy, instruction, curricular design, and assignments that chronologically advance students' achievement of expected learning outcomes.

Degree Qualifications Profile

The DQP is another grassroots-designed, outcomes-based framework that also focuses on equity, transparency, quality, and explicitness. The DQP was initiated and supported by the Lumina Foundation (2015) to contribute to its goal of increasing the "portion of Americans with high-quality degrees, certificates or other credentials to 60 percent by 2025." Importantly, the DQP initiative was led and developed by faculty and campus leaders to provide a national outcomes-based framework for what a quality degree represents in American higher education at the associate-, bachelor's-, and master's-degree levels. A quality degree integrates general education into student's major programs of study. Originally published in a beta version in 2011, this framework was field tested at over 400 institutions across the United States. Institutions' experiences from those field tests informed a second DQP draft released in January 2014 that was open for wider comment through March 2014 (Adelman, Ewell, Gaston, & Schneider, 2014). Based on stakeholder responses, campus experiences, and wider comments, a new DQP 2.0 was released in the fall of 2014, initiating another round of campus field-testing.

The DQP framework presents a broad set of outcomes, referred to as *proficiencies*, including most of the ELOs, further documenting the importance of students' abilities to apply and integrate their liberal learning outcomes in contexts well beyond the general education component of their undergraduate degrees. Use of the DQP also should "help students commit themselves to prepare fully for citizenship, for contributing to the economy and for the accomplishment of personal goals" (Lumina Foundation, 2014b, p. 10). The DQP Spiderweb Framework (Figure 2.2) illustrates that along with specialized knowledge in a major program of study, students attaining a degree also need to be able to demonstrate applied and collaborative learning; intellectual skills; broad, integrative knowledge; and civic and global learning.

Figure 2.2. The DQP Spiderweb Framework.

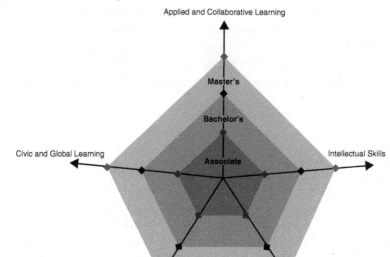

Source: Lumina Foundation. 2014b. *The Degree Qualifications Profile*. Reprinted with permission.

Using the VALUE rubrics to assess how well students achieve their liberal learning outcomes in multiple contexts, including in their majors, has become a practice among institutions that have adopted or field tested the DQP. For example, the rubrics provide a consistent way to assess students' progress toward achieving DQP intellectual skills such as analytic inquiry, information literacy, engaging diverse perspectives, quantitative fluency, and communication fluency. They provide a consistent way to assess civic learning and students' abilities to demonstrate integration and application of their learning in different contexts and across different assignments.

Similar to LEAP, the DQP emphasizes the value of students' abilities to apply their learning through, for example, "educational experiences rich in field-based projects, performances, investigative research, demonstrations, collaborations, and other learning-intensive activities" that all students should demonstrate (Lumina Foundation, 2011, p. 3). The DQP also focuses on the chronological importance of assignments that require students to address increasingly more complex tasks to achieve high-quality exit-level outcomes. From associate degree to master's degree, the DQP specifies leveled proficiency statements—levels of performance—requiring students to demonstrate them based on increasingly complicated tasks, thus requiring a close review of curricular design, sequencing, and chronological assignments intended to scaffold students' learning. For example, under one of the intellectual skills, information literacy, performance levels are described as follows:

- *At the associate level,* the student identifies, categorizes, evaluates and cites multiple information resources to create projects, papers, or performances in either a specialized field of study or with respect to a general theme within the arts and sciences.
- *At the bachelor's level,* the student locates, evaluates, incorporates, and properly cites multiple information resources in different media or different languages in projects, papers, or performances.Generates information through independent or collaborative inquiry and uses that information in a project, paper, or performance.
- *At the master's level,* the student provides evidence (through papers, projects, notebooks, computer files, or catalogues) of contributing to, expanding, evaluating, or refining the information base within the field of study. (Lumina Foundation, 2014b)

Sample assignments on the DQP Assignment Library, housed on the National Institute for Learning Outcomes Assessment site (NILOA) (www.assignmentlibrary.org) are helping others think through the design of their assignments. Case studies reporting on how institutions and organizations are using DQP are also available on the NILOA site (degreeprofileorg/ case-studies). Among those uses are taking a fresh look at how major programs integrate general education outcomes, examining how well department outcomes align with the DQP proficiencies, or facilitating transfer between two-year and four-year institutions.

One of those case studies is from a three-year AAC&U project launched in 2011—"Quality Collaboratives: Assessing and Reporting Degree Qualifications Profile Competencies in the Context of Transfer"—supported by grants from the Lumina Foundation and the William and Flora Hewlett Foundation. Using the DQP framework, this project brought together faculty from two- and four-year institutions in nine states to reach agreement about the desired outcomes that students need to demonstrate in their authentic work. The DQP promoted conversations among faculty in paired institutions about how curricular design and assignments across the two sets of institutions could be enhanced to ensure that students make a smooth transition to a four-year context. Assessment of student work using relevant VALUE rubrics was a means to identify common expectations for students' major program and general education outcomes. This effort has led to deeper agreement about what associate-degree students' exit-level work should demonstrate to ease their transition and the likelihood of their successful completion of a bachelor's degree. A more difficult issue to tackle was identifying the levels of achievement to satisfy agreed-upon degree outcomes. However, as the project summary states, "A starting point for transfer and assessment of learning competencies needs to focus attention on the importance of well-crafted assignments connected directly to the expected level of learning for each outcome" (AAC&U, 2014b; case study examples in Maki, 2015, pp. 37–39).

Field-Based, Professional, and Disciplinary Outcomes-Based Frameworks

In addition to long-standing specialized and national accreditors' outcomes-based frameworks, such as in nursing and other health professions, two major initiatives in this century are expanding the development or refinement of outcomes-based frameworks in other disciplines, professions, and fields of study. These initiatives are the Lumina Foundation's DQP/Tuning and the Department of Education's (DOE's) authorization in 2014 of a set of campus "experimental sites" to design and test new models for CBE programs and degrees. These efforts draw together faculty; administrators; external stakeholders, such as field experts and employers; and recently employed undergraduates. Convened to develop disciplinary, professional, or field-specific outcomes-based frameworks, contributors to these two efforts identify the most essential and relevant learning students need to transition into today's workforce.

DQP/Tuning

The DQP identifies overall degree proficiencies for all students. Tuning, an allied Lumina-foundation project initiated in 2008 and inspired by Tuning Educational Structures in Europe Association (Lumina Foundation, 2009), supports a finer-grained identification of current proficiencies for specific fields of study. Discipline-by-discipline projects led by faculty and organized by state higher education systems and field-based consortia across several states focus on identifying what students need to know and be able to do along their major program pathway using DQP proficiencies as markers. Organized by the Texas Higher Education Coordinating Board, Texas Tuning describes this commitment as follows: "Tuning provides an expected level of competency achievement at each step along the process of becoming a professional: expectations at the beginning of pre-professional study, at the beginning of professional study, and at the transition to practice" (Texas Higher Education Coordinating Board, n.d.). Achieving this field-based specificity requires engaging employers, faculty inside and outside of a field, and current and former students. The DQP represents expectations for a degree that include students' abilities to demonstrate their liberal learning outcomes; Tuning projects are designed within that DQP context.

Launched in 2009, Tuning projects are taking place across Texas, Kentucky, Minnesota, Indiana, and Utah. Civil and mechanical engineering, biology, chemistry, mathematics, chemical engineering, industrial engineering, biomedical engineering, graphic arts, history, physics, communications, business, nursing, social work, computer information systems and sciences, and management information systems are examples of fields being tuned. As is the case with the DQP, Lumina supports opportunities for faculty in these specific fields to meet with peers statewide to discuss shared expectations for student learning between two-year and four-year institutions (Lumina Foundation, 2009).

According to the Institute for Evidence-Based Change (2012), a Tuning initiative involves the following sequenced processes and substeps:

- Defining the discipline's core
    o Draft general degree profile, identify core concepts, draft competency statements, draft measurable student learning outcomes
- Mapping career pathways
    o Research student career destinations, develop careers pathway map
- Consulting stakeholders
    o Identify stakeholders, draft survey instruments or focus group protocols, gather stakeholder input
- Honing core competencies and learning outcomes
    o Review stakeholder feedback, review discipline core in light of feedback
- Implementing results locally and writing degree specifications
    o Identify departmental assets/priorities/missions, emphasize departmental distinctiveness, and write degree specifications for each degree level. (p. 6)

The American Historical Association (AHA) launched its Tuning project in 2012, bringing together history faculty from 2- and 4-year institutions from 70 institutions to develop consensus about "the skills, knowledge, and habits of mind that students develop in history courses and degree programs" (AHA, 2012). The first version of this project, the History Discipline Core, was published in 2012, revised in 2013, and updated again in 2016 (Box 2.1). The History Discipline Core begins by identifying what the discipline demands and requires of students. Within that context AHA recommends that history faculty adapt the six core categories and aligned learning outcomes listed in Box 2.1 for their individual campuses.

BOX 2.1
AHA Tuning Project: 2016 History Discipline Core

Discipline Profile and Core Concepts

History is the study of the human past as it is constructed and interpreted with human artifacts, written evidence, and oral traditions. It requires empathy for historical actors, respect for interpretive debate, and the skillful use of an evolving set of practices and tools.

As an inquiry into human experience, history demands that we consider the diversity of human experience across time and place.

As a public pursuit, history requires effective communication to make the past accessible; it informs and preserves collective memory; it is essential to active citizenship.

As a discipline, history requires a deliberative stance toward the past; the sophisticated use of information, evidence, and argumentation; and the ability to identify and explain continuity and change over time. Its professional ethics and standards demand peer review, citation, and acceptance of the provisional nature of knowledge.

Core Competencies and Learning Outcomes

History students can:

1. **Build historical knowledge.**
   a. Gather and contextualize information in order to convey both the particularity of past lives and the scale of human experience.
   b. Recognize how humans in the past shaped their own unique historical moments and were shaped by those moments.
   c. Develop a body of historical knowledge with breadth of time and place—as well as depth of detail—in order to discern context.
   d. Distinguish the past from our very different present.
2. **Develop historical methods.**
   a. Recognize history as an interpretive account of the human past— one that historians create in the present from surviving evidence.

    b. Collect, sift, organize, question, synthesize, and interpret complex material.

    c. Practice ethical historical inquiry that makes use of and acknowledges sources from the past as well as the scholars who have interpreted that past.

    d. Develop empathy toward people in the context of their distinctive historical moments.

3. Recognize the provisional nature of knowledge, the disciplinary preference for complexity, and the comfort with ambiguity that history requires.

    a. Welcome contradictory perspectives and data, which enable us to provide more accurate accounts and construct stronger arguments.

    b. Describe past events from multiple perspectives.

    c. Explain and justify multiple causes of complex events and phenomena using conflicting sources.

    d. Identify, summarize, appraise, and synthesize other scholars' historical arguments.

4. Apply the range of skills it takes to decode the historical record because of its incomplete, complex, and contradictory nature.

    a. Consider a variety of historical sources for credibility, position, perspective, and relevance.

    b. Evaluate historical arguments, explaining how they were constructed and might be improved.

    c. Revise analyses and narratives when new evidence requires it.

5. Create historical arguments and narratives.

    a. Generate substantive, open-ended questions about the past and develop research strategies to answer them.

    b. Craft well-supported historical narratives, arguments, and reports of research findings in a variety of media for a variety of audiences.

6. Use historical perspective as central to active citizenship.

    a. Apply historical knowledge and historical thinking to contemporary issues.

    b. Develop positions that reflect deliberation, cooperation, and diverse perspectives.

Source. From the American Historical Association Teaching Division, AHA History Tuning Project: Discipline Core. (2016). Used with permission. See https://www.historians.org/teaching-and-learning/tuning-the-history-discipline/2016-history-discipline-core

Competency-Based Programs and Degrees

Rooted in training programs in the 1960s, CBE expanded to accommodate non-traditional-age students in the 1970s and fueled the growth of online learning in the first decade of this century (Klein-Collins, 2013). Representing another outcomes-based framework, CBE identifies what students can do with the knowledge and skills they learn for a particular area of study. Typically, students' academic progress is demonstrated through mastery of more complex competencies documented in a record of their achievements, rather than grades. Students also proceed at different paces toward degree attainment based on specified competencies they may have developed already in their lives and ones they need to develop. Depending on which competencies need to be developed, some students take longer than others to reach mastery levels. Demonstration of mastery is key to CBE. This outcomes-based framework is yet another way in which growing numbers of institutions are chronologically assessing students' learning to assure students graduate having achieved equitable outcomes defining a quality program or degree. Different models of reporting students' competencies have evolved. Some are grounded in the traditional credit-hour standard while others are grounded in students' demonstration of self-paced mastery of competencies translated into credit-hour equivalency, required for DOE approval.

In 1999 Western Governors University (WGU) paved the way for competency-based online degree programs, providing working students with a more flexible way to progress toward degree attainment determined by "their demonstration of competence through carefully designed assessments and completion of a master portfolio, capstone, or both" (www.wgu.edu/wgu/credit/program560). Historically, however, the road toward the DOE's approval of proposed CBE programs has been rocky because of (a) unclear guidelines surrounding what institutions need to document about their proposed programs and (b) restrictions on eligibility for federal aid for CBE programs, making it difficult for many institutions to receive DOE approval. A confluence of recent developments pressed the DOE to waive some of the rules surrounding eligibility for federal aid and open the door to alternative models and modes of CBE delivery. Those developments include

- the national push to provide cost-effective alternative ways for students, especially working students, to study for and achieve a degree;
- the Obama administration's focus on increasing the number of Americans with postsecondary degrees or credentials through addressing affordability of a college education and its accessibility to working students; and
- surging institutional interest in offering CBE programs and degrees.

Two official developments opened the door for further development of CBE frameworks: President Obama's endorsement in his 2013 State of the Union address and the DOE's authorization of new approaches to CBE that same year. In a 2013 "Dear Colleague" letter, the DOE provides guidance for institutions "that wish to have direct assessment (competency-based) programs considered for Title IV, Higher Education Act (HEA) program eligibility." The letter also outlines how institutions can apply to the DOE for approval of competency-based programs that choose to measure student learning through direct assessment of students' performance, "including projects, papers, examinations, presentations, performances, and portfolios as measures of learning," instead of credit or clock hours (Federal Student Aid Office, 2013). When the DOE approved Southern New Hampshire University College's use of direct assessment degrees—competency-based, self-paced online degrees linked to student demonstration of increasingly complex compentencies, rather than seat time, credit hours, or grades—direct assesment CBE programs and degrees as a field was boosted. Soon thereafter, Capella University, the University of Wisconsin, Brandman University, Purdue University, and the University of Michigan were also approved (Fain, 2014). In July 2014 the Federal Student Aid Office announced it would waive existing rules for awarding federal aid for up to 40 institutions or consortia selected by DOE to serve as "experimental sites" to develop CBE approaches and modes of delivery that accommodate primarily working students who require a more flexible degree pathway than a traditional one (Federal Student Aid Office, 2014). That same month the House of Representatives' Education and Workforce Committee announced its Advancing Competency-Based Education Demonstration Project Act, "directing federal aid for up to 30 institutions selected by DOE to create competency-based education programs that reduce the cost of attaining a degree and are designed to accommodate students' financial and personal needs" (Education and the Workforce Committee, 2014). According to *Inside Higher Ed* in "Keeping Up With Competency," there are roughly 600 institutions now designing a CBE program or with one in place. That number is a major jump from the 52 institutions documented a year before (Fain, 2015b).

The emergence of different competency-based models, as well as ways of assessing learning—from standardized instruments or case studies or portfolios to the application of scoring rubrics to students' work or performances—led both the Lumina Foundation and the Bill & Melinda Gates Foundation to fund projects that have brought CBE institutions together to agree on a shared definition of *quality competency-based education* and then on principles and practices that assure that quality. In 2013 the Lumina Foundation called for applications from competency-based institutions to form a

Competency-Based Education Network (C-BEN). This three-year effort brings together selected teams from institutions with up-and-running competency-based degrees or programs to "address shared challenges to designing, developing and scaling competency-based degree programs" (Lumina Foundation, 2013). Across agreed-upon definitions, principles, and best practices there will be a range of competency-based models based, for example, on leveraging technology; credit for prior learning; and online, face-to-face, or blended learning options. Southern New Hampshire University hosts the network's site to disseminate results of this group's work and research (Fain, 2013). For institutions planning to design a competency degree or program, in 2015 the Bill & Melinda Gates Foundation funded an incubator project as one of its Next Generation Learning Challenges (NGLC) grant, managed by Educause. Institutions involved in this grant are focusing on designing competency-based models that draw on technology to "deliver and assess learning" to "expand access, affordability, and quality learning and degree attainment for more students" (Educause, 2015).

These two funded projects are critically important as ways to respond to or address concerns from the higher education community itself. The following concerns about CBE programs and degrees have been voiced from within higher education: (a) that CBE programs may focus on job preparation or certification at the expense of students' integration of and reflection on the relevance of the liberal learning component of their undergraduate education; and (b) that students in CBE programs may well focus more on ticking off competencies—perhaps from multiple educational providers—than on viewing and thinking about their learning within a coherent liberal arts undergraduate-degree framework. Both concerns focus on the significance of the general education component of students' education that provides them with the sets of capacities they will need not just for their immediate careers but also for future positions and for their roles as educated citizens. In contrast, the DQP and DQP/Tuning frameworks integrate LEAP outcomes and position students to integrate their liberal education into their major program of study, represented in Figure 2.2. Institutions using the DQP framework also draw on aligned VALUE rubrics to score student work that addresses general education outcomes in students' major programs of study.

In addition, CBE degrees grounded in the liberal arts can serve as models for others who plan to develop CBE programs and degrees. For example,

- Alverno College's well-known ability-based curriculum, consisting of eight liberal learning outcomes, prepares all students, regardless of their major program of study, "for a demanding and rapidly changing world" (Alverno College, 2015).

- Brandman University has worked with campus teams to integrate the ELOs and VALUE rubrics into its programs (Maki, 2015, pp. 35–36).
- College for America's CBE framework builds out from Southern New Hampshire University's existing associate- and bachelor's- degree programs grounded in the study of the liberal arts. Specifically, College for America incorporates the DQP framework, and both the DQP and LEAP focus on "solving real-world projects students complete, not courses they sit through" (Kazin, 2015a).

As former AAC&U president Carol Schneider said in 2015, the CBE "movement can be a 'potent force for good' if it is about applied learning— students' demonstrated ability to connect their learning with real-world challenges" (Fain, 2015a).

The Potential for Wider Application of Outcomes-Based Frameworks to Provide Coherence to Students' Diverse Degree Pathways

Students pursue different pathways to a degree, often accumulating credits from multiple sources. Aside from transfer of credits from two-year to four-year institutions, McCormick (2003) identified multi-institutional attendance patterns that students follow to bundle credits toward a degree. Included in those patterns (excluding direct transfer of students) are rebounding enrollment (students alternate course-taking at two or more institutions), concurrent enrollment (students take courses at two institutions simultaneously), and special program enrollment (students take most of their coursework at a host institution but also take advantage of unique programs at another institution).

Options for accumulating credits exist beyond attendance at one or more institutions. Credit for prior learning or on-the-job learning documented through credentialing organizations such as the American Council on Education (ACE) or the Council for Adult and Experiential Learning (CAEL) has long existed as another option. Continuing to expand options for credit in this century are courses and modules provided through other educational resources and alternative providers, such as Coursera, EdX, or Udacity. Credentialing organizations have awarded credit for learning through these options; however, institutions decide if they will accept those credits. In other instances, campuses themselves are piloting alternative providers' courses or modules or working directly with them to determine the creditworthiness of those providers' offerings (Masterson, 2013). Thus, layers of credentials from multiple institutions and other education providers may altogether contribute to the required number of credits a student needs for degree completion at a host institution. Underlying this credit-based system toward a degree is what McCormick (2003) describes as

> a sophisticated academic accounting system that has grown up around portable course credits and presumed equivalency, facilitating transfer between institutions and students' ability to assemble educational programs from coursework at any number of institutions. Whether this accumulation of educational threads amounts to a loose patchwork or a rich tapestry is largely up to the student. . . . When the only currency is the credit hour, the only question becomes one of course equivalency. Important questions about the coherence and sequence of an educational program go largely unasked. These are conversations that faculty need to have, even in the absence of extensive student mobility between institutions. But mobility makes them all the more urgent. (p. 23)

More than a list of degree and program courses and credits, often assembled from several institutions, credentialors, and education providers, the DQP and LEAP expect students to demonstrate their learning, apply it, and integrate it, not just check off courses completed and passed. Widened use of the DQP framework with its integration of ELOs and aligned scoring rubrics across education providers and credentialors could address institutions' often-diminished view of the quality or rigor represented in transfer credits.

Several projects serve as models for widening the use of the DQP, ELOs, and the VALUE rubrics for purposes of equitably validating students' learning. AAC&U's and the Lumina Foundation's funded projects focused on two-year transfer represent one example. Reducing uncertainty about what coursework will transfer and how well students are prepared to transfer has been based on discussions and agreement among faculty from both types of institutions about what students need to demonstrate as opposed to relying solely on students' grades (this volume, pp. 37–38).

Two other multi-institutional projects built on collaboration have drawn on ELOs and VALUE rubrics to document students' achievement for transfer:

1. Western Interstate Commission for Higher Education's development of an Interstate Passport that documents students' proficiencies for transfer

to four-year institutions in California, Hawaii, North Dakota, Oregon, and Utah were informed by the ELOs and VALUE rubrics.

2. Metropolitan Higher Education Consortium's use of the Written Communication VALUE rubric across its 12 higher education institutions in the Southland regions of the Chicago Metropolitan area aligns expectations across those campuses and identifies patterns of underperformance that students need to improve (see also Maki, 2015, p. 36).

The DQP, ELOs, and the VALUE rubrics have informed Open SUNY's Global Learning Qualifications Profile, "designed to assist students to document their verifiable college/university-level learning for academic credit and to provide an academic framework for evaluators to evaluate student learning" (SUNY Empire State College, n.d.). The framework clusters learning into three overarching constructs that subdivide into eight learning domains. Students' learning is achieved through open educational sources (OESs), massive open online courses (MOOCs), and prior experiential learning (Ford, 2014, p. 5).

Kate Ford (2014), director of the University of Maryland's Center for Innovation in Learning and Student Success, views the DQP as a national qualifications framework to improve "transparency, transferability, and recognition of degree credentials" as well as serve the needs "for a highly educated and geographically mobile workforce" (p. 6). Without an agreed-upon framework that is based on students' demonstration of their learning, bundling of credits toward a degree will remain the goal, challenging the coherence and integrity of a degree and separating students from the possibility of continuous engagement in their learning. In the words of Schneider and Schoenberg (1999), "Educational goals should not simply be imparted to students; they need to become a continuing framework for students' educational planning, assessments, and self-assessment" (p. 35).

Both the institution-level outcomes-based frameworks, LEAP and DQP, and recent developments in disciplinary, professional, and field-based outcomes frameworks—through DQP/Tuning and expansion of CBE models—are steering our campuses away from credits and grades as measures of learning to students' performance in their authentic work as the accurate measure of their learning. Developed through collaboration, outcomes-based frameworks provide an institution and its programs with the means to monitor our diverse students' progress as well as address patterns of underperformance when they occur and as they persist. Over time, these frameworks have the potential to assure coherence across the diverse pathways students pursue to achieve a degree.

Chapter 3 identifies the sets of core learner-centered commitments that stretch across outcomes-based frameworks to provide clarity and coherence to students' pathways as well as support real-time student assessment. That approach to assessment involves continuously gauging students' progress toward attaining a high-quality degree to prepare students equitably for twenty-first-century demands and opportunities.

Critical Thinking VALUE Rubric

The VALUE rubrics were developed by teams of faculty experts representing colleges and universities across the United States through a process that examined many existing campus rubrics and related documents for each learning outcome and incorporated additional feedback from faculty. The rubrics articulate fundamental criteria for each learning outcome, with performance descriptors demonstrating progressively more sophisticated levels of attainment. The rubrics are intended for institutional-level use in evaluating and discussing student learning, not for grading. The core expectations articulated in all 15 of the VALUE rubrics can and should be translated into the language of individual campuses, disciplines, and even courses. The utility of the VALUE rubrics is to position learning at all undergraduate levels within a basic framework of expectations such that evidence of learning can be shared nationally through a common dialog and understanding of student success.

Definition

Critical thinking is a habit of mind characterized by the comprehensive exploration of issues, ideas, artifacts, and events before accepting or formulating an opinion or conclusion.

Framing Language

This rubric is designed to be transdisciplinary, reflecting the recognition that success in all disciplines requires habits of inquiry and analysis that share common attributes. Further, research suggests that successful critical thinkers from all disciplines increasingly need to be able to apply those habits in various and changing situations encountered in all walks of life.

This rubric is designed for use with many different types of assignments and the suggestions here are not an exhaustive list of possibilities. Critical thinking can be demonstrated in assignments that require students to complete analyses of text, data, or issues. Assignments that cut across presentation mode might be especially useful in some fields. If insight into the process components of critical thinking (e.g., how information sources were evaluated regardless of whether they were included in the product) is important, assignments focused on student reflection might be especially illuminating.

Glossary

The definitions that follow were developed to clarify terms and concepts used in this rubric only:

- *Ambiguity:* Information that may be interpreted in more than one way.
- *Assumptions:* Ideas, conditions, or beliefs (often implicit or unstated) that are "taken for granted or accepted as true without proof" (www .dictionary.reference.com/browse/assumptions).
- *Context:* The historical, ethical, political, cultural, environmental, or circumstantial settings or conditions that influence and complicate the consideration of any issues, ideas, artifacts, and events.
- *Literal meaning:* Interpretation of information exactly as stated. For example, "she was green with envy" would be interpreted to mean that her skin was green.
- *Metaphor:* Information that is (intended to be) interpreted in a non-literal way. For example, "she was green with envy" is intended to convey an intensity of emotion, not a skin color.

Critical Thinking VALUE Rubric

Reprinted with the permission of the Association of American Colleges & Universities. For more information, please contact value@aacu.org.

Definition

Critical thinking is a habit of mind characterized by the comprehensive exploration of issues, ideas, artifacts, and events before accepting or formulating an opinion or conclusion.

Evaluators are encouraged to assign a zero to any work sample or collection of work that does not meet benchmark (cell one)-level performance.

	Capstone	Milestones		Benchmark
	4	3	2	1
Explanation of issues	Issue/problem to be considered critically is stated clearly and described comprehensively, delivering all relevant information necessary for full understanding.	Issue/problem to be considered critically is stated, described, and clarified so that understanding is not seriously impeded by omissions.	Issue/problem to be considered critically is stated but description leaves some terms undefined, ambiguities unexplored, boundaries undetermined, and/or backgrounds unknown.	Issue/problem to be considered critically is stated without clarification or description.
Evidence *Selecting and using information to investigate a point of view or conclusion*	Information is taken from source(s) with enough interpretation/evaluation to develop a comprehensive analysis or synthesis. Viewpoints of experts are questioned thoroughly.	Information is taken from source(s) with enough interpretation/evaluation to develop a coherent analysis or synthesis. Viewpoints of experts are subject to questioning.	Information is taken from source(s) with some interpretation/evaluation, but not enough to develop a coherent analysis or synthesis. Viewpoints of experts are taken as mostly fact, with little questioning.	Information is taken from source(s) without any interpretation/evaluation. Viewpoints of experts are taken as fact, without question.

A|A
C|U

Association
of American
Colleges and
Universities

(Continues)

Critical Thinking VALUE Rubric (Continued)

	Capstone 4	Milestones		Benchmark 1
		3	2	
Influence of context and assumptions	Thoroughly (systematically and methodically) analyzes own and others' assumptions and carefully evaluates the relevance of contexts when presenting a position.	Identifies own and others' assumptions and several relevant contexts when presenting a position.	Questions some assumptions. Identifies several relevant contexts when presenting a position. May be more aware of other's assumptions than one's own (or vice versa).	Shows an emerging awareness of present assumptions (sometimes labels assertions as assumptions). Begins to identify some contexts when presenting a position.
Student's position (perspective, thesis/ hypothesis)	Specific position (perspective, thesis/hypothesis) is imaginative, taking into account the complexities of an issue. Limits of position (perspective, thesis/ hypothesis) are acknowledged. Others' points of view are synthesized within position (perspective, thesis/ hypothesis).	Specific position (perspective, thesis/hypothesis) takes into account the complexities of an issue. Others' points of view are acknowledged within position (perspective, thesis/ hypothesis).	Specific position (perspective, thesis/hypothesis) acknowledges different sides of an issue.	Specific position (perspective, thesis/hypothesis) is stated, but is simplistic and obvious.
Conclusions and related outcomes (implications and consequences)	Conclusions and related outcomes (consequences and implications) are logical and reflect student's informed evaluation and ability to place evidence and perspectives discussed in priority order.	Conclusion is logically tied to a range of information, including opposing viewpoints; related outcomes (consequences and implications) are identified clearly.	Conclusion is logically tied to information (because information is chosen to fit the desired conclusion); some related outcomes (consequences and implications) are identified clearly.	Conclusion is inconsistently tied to some of the information discussed; related outcomes (consequences and implications) are oversimplified.

T he VALUE rubrics were developed by teams of faculty experts representing colleges and universities across the United States through a process that examined many existing campus rubrics and related documents for each learning outcome and incorporated additional feedback from faculty. The rubrics articulate fundamental criteria for each learning outcome, with performance descriptors demonstrating progressively more sophisticated levels of attainment. The rubrics are intended for institutional-level use in evaluating and discussing student learning, not for grading. The core expectations articulated in all 15 of the VALUE rubrics can and should be translated into the language of individual campuses, disciplines, and even courses. The utility of the VALUE rubrics is to position learning at all undergraduate levels within a basic framework of expectations such that evidence of learning can be shared nationally through a common dialog and understanding of student success.

Definition

Integrative learning is an understanding and a disposition that a student builds across the curriculum and cocurriculum, from making simple connections among ideas and experiences to synthesizing and transferring learning to new, complex situations within and beyond the campus.

Framing Language

Fostering students' abilities to integrate learning—across courses, over time, and between campus and community life—is one of the most important goals and challenges for higher education. Initially, students connect previous learning to new classroom learning. Later, significant knowledge within individual disciplines serves as the foundation, but integrative learning goes

Reprinted with the permission of the Association of American Colleges & Universities. For more information, please contact value@aacu.org.

beyond academic boundaries. Indeed, integrative experiences often occur as learners address real-world problems, unscripted and sufficiently broad, to require multiple areas of knowledge and multiple modes of inquiry, offering multiple solutions and benefiting from multiple perspectives. Integrative learning also involves internal changes in the learner. These internal changes, which indicate growth as a confident, lifelong learner, include the ability to adapt one's intellectual skills, to contribute in a wide variety of situations, and to understand and develop individual purpose, values, and ethics. Developing students' capacities for integrative learning is central to personal success, social responsibility, and civic engagement in today's global society. Students face a rapidly changing and increasingly connected world where integrative learning becomes not just a benefit, but a necessity.

Because integrative learning is about making connections, this learning may not be as evident in traditional academic artifacts such as research papers and academic projects unless the student, for example, is prompted to draw implications for practice. These connections often surface, however, in reflective work, self-assessment, or creative endeavors of all kinds. Integrative assignments foster learning between courses or by connecting courses to experientially based work. Work samples or collections of work that include such artifacts give evidence of integrative learning. Faculty are encouraged to look for evidence that the student connects the learning gained in classroom study to learning gained in real-life situations that are related to other learning experiences, extracurricular activities, or work. Through integrative learning, students pull together their entire experience inside and outside of the formal classroom; thus, artificial barriers between formal study and informal or tacit learning become permeable. Integrative learning, whatever the context or source, builds upon connecting both theory and practice toward a deepened understanding.

Assignments to foster such connections and understanding could include, for example, composition papers that focus on topics from biology, economics, or history; mathematics assignments that apply mathematical tools to important issues and require written analysis to explain the implications and limitations of the mathematical treatment; or art history presentations that demonstrate aesthetic connections between selected paintings and novels. In this regard, some majors (e.g., interdisciplinary majors or problem-based field studies) seem to inherently evoke characteristics of integrative learning and result in work samples or collections of work that significantly demonstrate this outcome. However, fields of study that require accumulation of extensive and high-consensus content knowledge (e.g., accounting, engineering, or chemistry) also involve the kinds of complex and integrative constructions (e.g., ethical dilemmas and social consciousness) that seem to be highlighted so extensively in self-reflection in arts and humanities, but they may be embedded in individual performances and less evident. The key in the development of such work samples or collections of work will be in designing structures that include artifacts and reflective writing or feedback that support students' examination of their learning and give evidence that, as graduates, they will extend their integrative abilities into the challenges of personal, professional, and civic life.

Glossary

The definitions that follow were developed to clarify terms and concepts used in this rubric only.

- *Academic Knowledge*: Disciplinary learning; learning from academic study, texts, and so on.
- *Content*: The information conveyed in the work samples or collections of work.
- *Contexts*: Actual or simulated situations in which a student demonstrates learning outcomes. New and challenging contexts encourage students to stretch beyond their current frames of reference.
- *Cocurriculum*: A parallel component of the academic curriculum that is in addition to formal classroom (student government, community service, residence hall activities, student organizations, etc.).
- *Experience*: Learning that takes place in a setting outside of the formal classroom, such as workplace, service-learning site, internship site, or another location.
- *Form*: The external frameworks in which information and evidence are presented, ranging from choices for particular work sample or collection of works (e.g., a research paper, PowerPoint, video recording) to choices in make-up of the eportfolio.
- *Performance*: A dynamic and sustained act that brings together knowing and doing (creating a painting, solving an experimental design problem, developing a public relations strategy for a business, etc.); performance makes learning observable.
- *Reflection*: A metacognitive act of examining a performance in order to explore its significance and consequences.
- *Self-Assessment*: Describing, interpreting, and judging a performance based on stated or implied expectations followed by planning for further learning.

Integrative Learning VALUE Rubric

Reprinted with the permission of the Association of American Colleges & Universities. For more information, please contact value@aacu.org.

Definition

Integrative learning is an understanding and a disposition that a student builds across the curriculum and cocurriculum, from making simple connections among ideas and experiences to synthesizing and transferring learning to new, complex situations within and beyond the campus.

Evaluators are encouraged to assign a zero to any work sample or collection of work that does not meet benchmark (cell one)-level performance.

	Capstone 4	Milestones 3	Milestones 2	Benchmark 1
Connections to Experience *Connects relevant experience and academic knowledge*	Meaningfully **synthesizes** connections among experiences outside of the formal classroom (including life experiences and academic experiences such as internships and travel abroad) to **deepen understanding** of fields of study and to broaden own points of view.	Effectively **selects and develops** examples of life experiences, drawn from a variety of contexts (e.g., family life, artistic participation, civic involvement, work experience), to **illuminate** concepts/theories/frameworks of fields of study.	**Compares** life experiences and academic knowledge to infer differences, as well as similarities, and **acknowledges perspectives** other than own.	**Identifies** connections between life experiences and those academic texts and ideas **perceived as similar and related** to own interests.
Connections to Discipline *Sees (makes) connections across disciplines, perspectives*	Independently creates wholes out of multiple parts (synthesizes) or draws conclusions by combining examples, facts, or theories from more than one field of study or perspective.	Independently connects examples, facts, or theories from more than one field of study or perspective.	When prompted, connects examples, facts, or theories from more than one field of study or perspective.	When prompted, presents examples, facts, or theories from more than one field of study or perspective.

Transfer *Adapts and applies skills, abilities, theories, or methodologies gained in one situation to new situations*	Adapts and applies, independently, skills, abilities, theories, or methodologies gained in one situation to solve **difficult problems or explore complex issues in original ways.**	Adapts and applies skills, abilities, theories, or methodologies gained in one situation to new situations to **solve problems or explore issues.**	Uses skills, abilities, theories, or methodologies gained in one situation in a new situation **to contribute to understanding of problems or issues.**	Uses, in a basic way, skills, abilities, theories, or methodologies gained in one situation **in a new situation.**
Integrated Communication	Fulfills the assignment(s) by choosing a format, language, or graph (or other visual representation) **in ways that enhance meaning,** making clear the interdependence of language and meaning, thought, and expression.	Fulfills the assignment(s) by choosing a format, language, or graph (or other visual representation) **to explicitly connect content and form,** demonstrating awareness of purpose and audience.	Fulfills the assignment(s) by choosing a format, language, or graph (or other visual representation) that **connects in a basic way** what is being communicated (content) with how it is said (form).	Fulfills the assignment(s) (i.e., to produce an essay, a poster, a video, a PowerPoint presentation, etc.) **in an appropriate form.**
Reflection and Self-Assessment *Demonstrates a developing sense of self as a learner, building on prior experiences to respond to new and challenging contexts (may be evident in self-assessment, reflective, or creative work)*	Envisions a future self and possibly makes plans that build on past experiences that have occurred across multiple and diverse contexts.	Evaluates changes in own learning over time, recognizing complex contextual factors (e.g., works with ambiguity and risk, deals with frustration, considers ethical frameworks).	Articulates strengths and challenges (within specific performances or events) to increase effectiveness in different contexts (through increased self-awareness).	Describes own performances with general descriptors of success and failure.

3

THE CANVAS OF CORE LEARNER-CENTERED COMMITMENTS THAT STRETCHES ACROSS AN OUTCOMES-BASED FRAMEWORK

N ational outcomes-based frameworks—along with developments in disciplinary, professional, field-specific, and national and specialized accreditors' outcomes-based frameworks—establish the substructure to build real-time student assessment. These frameworks provide institutions and their programs with a foundation upon which to keep students on track and measurably narrow achievement and graduation gaps. They also specify what all students should be able to demonstrate upon graduation. How well institutions and their programs intentionally support and monitor students' equitable progress, however, requires developing a canvas of interdependent learner-centered commitments. These commitments together stretch across an outcomes-based framework. Chapter 3 identifies a set of core learner-centered commitments to guide examining your current set of commitments. The interdependency of these commitments provides coherence to students' degree and program pathways and positions students to make sense of what they have learned in relation to what they are currently learning. Without this canvas, assessment remains an uneven commitment to all students. In the first part of this chapter, I identify and describe the five core learner-centered commitments. A case study in the second part of this chapter illustrates how shortcomings in one or more of these commitments lead to inequitable attention to all currently enrolled students.

Five Core Learner-Centered Commitments

Presented here are five commitments that work interdependently to form a canvas of learner-centered commitments that stretches across an outcomes-based framework. Without this canvas, it is unlikely that the institution and its programs will remain continuously informed about and respond in a timely fashion to students' equitable progress.

Commitment 1: A Shared Commitment to Close Existing Achievement and Graduation Gaps Measurably

Inequities in student success are bound to occur unless a stated and shared commitment exists to close achievement and graduation gaps between historically represented and underrepresented students. This is the the first learner-centered commitment. Closing gaps is a continuous and intentional learner-centered commitment among all constituencies at an institution. Institutions focused on increasingly closing those gaps set measurable, often annual, goals to achieve that end, coupled with action plans. That pledge originates with institutional or system leaders and extends to academic and administrative leaders, faculty, and all professional contributors to student learning.

Lessons learned from multi-institutional projects focused on measurably improving persistence, achievement, and graduation rates for historically underrepresented students underscore the significance of institution or system leaders' essential role in anchoring a shared commitment to these ends. For example, Yeado, Haycock, Johnstone, and Chaplot (2014) reported major findings of an eight-institution project funded by the Education Trust focused on closing achievement and graduation gaps. The authors concluded that among the most important findings of this project "is the role of campus leadership—including the president but especially the provost—in helping to make student success a high, institution-wide priority" (p. 2).

Closing gaps in achievement and graduation rates is based on concerted and interdependent efforts across an institution focused on student success. Reporting on the eight universities' efforts to narrow and close achievement gaps, Yeado and colleagues (2014) identified the common need across those institutions for systematic reporting on student progress from multiple sources and at multiple times, beginning at students' point of entry. Several institutions, for example, identified early credit-bearing high-enrollment courses that had high dismissal, withdrawal, and failure (DWF) rates. Among the courses that institutions identified were required mathematics courses. DWF rates across all student cohorts were high; however, the rates for minorities were the highest. Instead of viewing those results as inevitable, institutions directed immediate efforts toward redesigning high-risk early credit-bearing courses such as mathematics. For example, Georgia State University redesigned early credit-bearing mathematics courses by replacing traditional classroom instruction with blended learning in a computer lab and staffing labs with graduate assistants available 24/7 to assist students as they solve problems. The use of on-demand graduate assistants recognizes the importance of developing interventions as students solve problems, so that students stay on track rather than give up (Yeado et al., 2014, pp. 4–5). In the redesign of its early credit-bearing math course, the University of Alabama adapted Georgia State University's model and reported that the Black-White gap in performance "completely disappeared." In addition, the university reported that its previous 50% success rates swiftly increased as well (Yeado et al., 2014, pp. 6–7). Often what lifts one cohort lifts other cohorts.

Lessons shared from another multi-institutional project, the University Innovation Alliance (UIA), substantiate the importance of a shared commitment across an institution to historically underrepresented students' success. Supported by grants from the Bill & Melinda Gates Foundation, the Lumina Foundation, and matching grants from participating institutions themselves, UIA is a coalition of 11 large public research universities located across the United States. Altogether these institutions are focused on developing practices that increase the achievement and graduation rates of their socioeconomically diverse student cohorts. These institutions have identified graduation targets for traditionally underrepresented students as well as institution-wide strategies to achieve those goals. A shared belief across participating institutions in this coalition is that when institutions work together, not alone, they are able to develop, pilot test, and take to scale effective practices across multiple institutions. These institutions understand the need to implement and coordinate a range of strategies or practices to achieve their goals and to keep internal stakeholders continually informed about students' progress. Among these practices are initial reports on students' academic achievement in summer bridge programs, followed by multipronged chronological efforts such as targeted advising, early warning systems, supplemental instruction, tutoring, or the use of predictive analytics—technology platforms that use data collection techniques to identify students who are underperforming (see also chapter 5, p. 133). Developing action plans to accompany shared commitments and goals to close "attainment gaps for traditionally underrepresented populations" is at the core of the pledge governors make when their states join Complete College America. Participating states agree to prioritize college completion and implement a set of agreed-upon actions, such as using common yardsticks to measure student progress (Complete College America, n.d.).

Commitment 2: Agreement on the Language of Outcomes and Scoring Rubrics to Continuously Identify Patterns of Performance and Underperformance

The second learner-centered commitment involves two linked efforts: agreement on an outcomes-based framework for general education and students' majors, such as those identified in chapter 2, and agreement on the language of scoring rubrics or other metrics to assess and report on students' equitable progress toward achieving those outcomes at high levels.

Outcomes-Based Frameworks

Carrying out a comprehensive commitment to improve persistence, achievement, and graduation gaps is a multipronged effort. Working in conjunction with other institutional practices and strategies that support students' success, such as the redesign of high-risk courses or just-in-time advising, outcomes-based frameworks provide the foundation for an institution and its programs to monitor currently enrolled students' equitable academic progress. Preceding adoption of these frameworks, however, faculty members and other contributors to student learning must discuss the language of outcomes-based frameworks. Important questions to raise in these discussions include: How well does the language of an outcomes-based framework align with our institution- and program-level language or current outcomes? How could we align our existing institution- or program-level outcomes with the language of a framework? Adopting an existing outcomes-based framework full-cloth without discussion often leads to a forced or uncomfortable institutional fit. A lack of agreement at the institution and program levels about a shared set of outcomes encompassed in an outcomes-based framework may also cause some educators to withdraw from the essential participation necessary to track all students' learning. For many institutions, however, campus discussions focused on the Degree Qualifications Profile (DQP; see Ewell, 2013) or Liberal Education and America's Promise (LEAP) outcomes provide a long-awaited opportunity to take a fresh look at the relevance of their general education programs and students' major programs of study in relation to the twenty-first-century needs identified in chapter 1. For example, identifying gaps between DQP or LEAP outcomes and an institution's general education outcomes leads to recalibrating existing outcomes or identifying new ones. Some institutions choose to adapt the language of established outcomes-based frameworks to better suit their current general education or program-level outcomes or internal language. Further, reaching agreement about outcomes may also involve including other mission-specific outcomes that an institution and its programs value. Without an agreed-upon outcomes-based framework, there will be uneven attention paid to students' progress toward achieving the institution's general education outcomes or those of its programs.

The set of agreed-upon physical science outcomes shown in Case 3.1 represents the disciplinary depth and breadth students must demonstrate in Utah State University's general education curriculum. Incorporated into these outcomes are also other liberal learning outcomes, such as writing, speaking, information literacy, and quantitative reasoning. Disciplinary courses approved for general education provide students options; yet across those options faculty assess the same outcomes to assure there is even attention to all students' achievement.

CASE 3.1.
Development of Disciplinary Depth and Breadth in Utah State University's General Education Curriculum

To ensure that students achieve both disciplinary depth and breadth in the university's general education curriculum, faculty at Utah State University have developed a shared set of outcomes that students need to demonstrate for upper and lower level disciplinary courses. These outcomes also include other liberal learning outcomes such as writing, speaking, quantitative reasoning, and information literacy. For example, all courses approved for general education in the physical sciences must demonstrate how they develop students' abilities to

- understand how the enterprise of science works (i.e., erecting testable hypotheses, refining hypotheses, reproducing results);
- understand key laws, concepts, and processes that govern physical systems;
- utilize quantitative methods to address a process or principle (i.e., computation); interpret results (e.g., in a graph or table); and understand the meaning of accuracy, uncertainty, precision, and error;
- evaluate the credibility of various sources of information about science-related issues;
- use written or visual communication to demonstrate knowledge of scientific findings; and
- examine the relationship of the science learned to societal issues (e.g., sustainability). (See www.usu.edu/provost/academic_programs/geduc_univstud/doc/USU%20General%20Education-Physical%20Sciences.pdf)

Articulating shared outcomes for students' general education disciplinary learning has learner-centered advantages for students, faculty, and the institution.

Students: Students can choose among courses offered in a discipline because they all have commonly agreed-upon outcomes as well as aligned proficiency goals against which faculty assess students' levels of performance.

Faculty: Faculty have shared goals and outcomes for assessing student work. These goals and outcomes allow them to identify assessable artifacts across disciplinary courses, throwing patterns of underperformance in relief.

Institution: The institution assures that students have equitable opportunities to learn about and use what they learn in a discipline, including other generic general education outcomes, such as writing and speaking. That is, approved general education courses reflect a shared commitment to what all students should learn across the range of general courses they select. Moreover, disciplines that make use of general education courses know what those courses do, and do not, provide students.

Note. The text for this institutional example was collaboratively developed between Norman Jones and the author through personal communication on February 29, 2016. Norman Jones, professor of history, served as director of general education and curricular integration at Utah State University at the time the university's outcomes were developed.

For all students, and particularly those who are the first of their generation to attend college, public dissemination of institution- and program-level outcomes in online and print catalogs specifies what a postsecondary education aims for them to achieve. Until this century that was not historically a higher education practice.

Criteria and Standards of Judgment

Outcomes-based frameworks provide an institution and its programs with a shared macro-level language. Determining what quality performance looks like in students' authentic work and tracking students' progress toward demonstrating quality, however, require another level of collaborative agreement. Increasingly, as illustrated in examples described in chapter 2 (pp. 32–35) institutions are using or adapting the Association of American Colleges & Universities' (AAC&U's) Valid Assessment of Learning in Undergraduate Education (VALUE) rubrics as the shared means to assess students' equitable development and achievement of general education outcomes. Agreeing to use relevant VALUE rubrics or to adapt them in relation to an institution's mission is another major learner-centered commitment. It follows on the heels of reaching agreement on the language of outcome statements. That is, faculty and all others who contribute to students' general education outcomes need to agree on the essential sets of criteria that will be consistently used across the institution to assess students' equitable achievement of those outcomes. In addition, individual programs need to develop or adapt existing scoring rubrics such as those used in competency-based education programs or in programs that have gone through the DQP/Tuning process. Faculty in disciplines or fields of study often customize VALUE rubrics, such as the critical thinking rubric or the written communication rubric, to suit their programs. Agreeing on the language of scoring rubrics becomes a shared means to

- monitor students' equitable progress;
- provide consistent feedback to students, holding them accountable for their learning and future improvements; and
- prompt students' self-reflection on their progress, often in the presence of a trusted other, such as an adviser.

Absent national examples of scoring rubrics, it is possible to develop them internally based on closely examining samples of near-graduation student work, representing high to low levels of achievement. Criteria and standards of judgment can be derived from these leveled examples based on current students' exit-level performance. These rubrics should then be pilot tested on other sets of student examples to assure the validity of the language of criteria and performance levels. Some rubrics identify milestone achievement levels as a way to more closely monitor and report expected performance levels that trigger timely interventions to improve student performance. Establishing a common language is necessary to develop interrater reliability across scorers to assess student work assigned in different contexts and at different levels of complexity. Just as national efforts to achieve interrater reliability are conducted through rounds of scoring examples of student work, as illustrated in the Multi-State Collaborative to Advance Learning Outcomes Assessment (MSC) project in chapter 2, rounds of scoring should also be conducted across a campus or a program. That practice builds scoring agreement among peers based on discussions about how students do or do not demonstrate specific criteria at different levels of achievement. Scorers using handheld clickers facilitate the process of achieving interrater reliability across large groups. On-screen results identify areas of disagreement that warrant further discussion and recalibration. Developing interrater reliability is key to reporting course-based and experience-based results that serve as formative evidence of students' equitable progress toward degree attainment in real-time student assessment.

Agreement on the language of scoring rubrics does not exclude the possibility that additional course- or program-specific criteria might be included in them. It does mean that an agreed-upon final set of essential criteria should be used consistently to assess all students' progress toward high-quality, exit-level achievement. Without that agreement, students' work will be assessed unevenly based on each individual's weighting or grading systems. Compared to grades and credit hours earned, scoring rubrics also provide finer-grained documentation of student achievement based on students' authentic work in a range of contexts. Unless an agreed-upon grading practice exists across an institution or even across a program, grades typically reflect educators' individual practices. For example, averaging each student's grades might be one way to determine final grades. Weighting students' performance on assignments might be another way. Including class participation or extra credit is yet another among the many ways to arrive at students' final grades. With an agreed-upon set of outcomes and aligned rubrics, such as those represented in the VALUE rubrics, a campus and its programs establish a shared vocabulary to assess students' chronological performance and thereby identify and address in real time the barriers or obstacles that students face as they demonstrate outcomes. For some programs, standardized tests and licensure examinations provide national benchmarks for student performance. Yet, to increase the likelihood that students will perform well on these instruments, faculty and other professional educators need to know how well students are advancing course-by-course or experience-by-experience to perform at externally established exit levels. Agreeing on a set of scoring rubrics to track students' progress becomes a granular means of targeting areas of weakness in student work that need to be addressed well before students sit for an exam.

Commitment 3: Coherence Across the Curriculum, Cocurriculum, and Other Educational Experiences

Together, the language of outcomes and that of scoring rubrics directly shape the design and even sequencing of curricula, cocurricula, and other chronological educational opportunities, ultimately creating the third learner-centered commitment: coherence. This commitment involves determining how the components of students' undergraduate learning—courses, educational experiences, programs, and services—concomitantly advance currently enrolled students to achieve high-quality exit-level outcomes. Across most campuses, curricular and cocurricular maps are visual representations of coherence, identifying when, where, and even how students learn. These maps may also identify the methods of assessment used in courses or educational experiences and even the level of expected performance— particularly in mastery-based learning frameworks. The maps can also help in pinpointing chronological gaps in student opportunities to continue to practice and apply their learning and receive feedback on their levels of performance. Limited or unequal opportunities for a group of students to receive feedback from peers or educators and self-reflect on their progress toward high-quality exit-level performance should be addressed in curricular and cocurricular design to assure that all students, not some students, have equal opportunities to improve their achievement levels and advance to degree completion. For example, a program that does not intentionally provide chronological opportunities for students to reason mathematically or to write across its curriculum and receive feedback on their progress disadvantages those students from progressing toward achieving the institution's high-quality achievement standards for those two general education outcomes. Relying on one course to advance students to a high achievement level assumes that all students can achieve that level at the same time or that students will sustain that level of learning over long gaps in time—from first year to the second, third, or fourth year, for example.

Curricular and cocurricular maps, or more learner-centered versions of them, are also important for students to see. They document when and where students will continue to build and draw on their learning along their undergraduate pathway. Thus, they also contribute to students' understanding of the significance and relevance of learning outcomes in multiple contexts beyond a required or lower-level course. A commitment to students' achievement of high-quality exit-level outcomes extends beyond students' learning in a single course or through a single experience. Thus, closely gauging students' progress along their undergraduate pathway and in multiple contexts is key to understanding how well equipped they are for what lies ahead. Are students attaining a level of performance that will enable them to be successful as they progress? Norman Jones's axiom to faculty says it best: "A student's next employer is the professor in the next class. A student leaving your course should be prepared to succeed in the next course" (N. Jones, personal communication, February 29, 2016).

AAC&U's recent project, General Education Maps and Markers (GEMS), another LEAP initiative, illustrates the importance of developing curricular/ cocurricular coherence in redesigned general education programs that enable students chronologically to extend, build on, and apply their general education learning in their major programs of study. In 2015 the organization launched an initiative bringing together a set of two- and four-year public and private institutions to reform their current general education models into more purposeful learner-centered ones. Specifically these models will be "designed in ways that clearly articulate for students how and where they can develop and demonstrate" their general education outcomes across their undergraduate pathways (AAC&U, 2015b, p. 15). These learner-centered models will demonstrate efficacious ways in which students

- learn and apply their liberal learning outcomes in redesigned general education programs that actively engage students in applying that learning in "relevant contexts such as service learning, cocurricular and community activities and digital environments"; and
- continue to hone those outcomes in their major programs of study, providing diverse and more complex contexts that equitably prepare students to see the purpose and relevance of their liberal learning for this century. (AAC&U, 2015b, p. 13)

AAC&U's GEMS project identifies coherence as essential to the design of general education programs: "Student success is more likely to be achieved through a coherent program of study that integrates academic, co-curricular, and community work and involves clear and coherent educational pathways and meaningful problem-based inquiry and analysis" (AAC&U, 2015b, p. 9). A guideline for institutions involved in the project also asks them to examine their programs' chronological coherence: "Does the general education program clearly map and guide students along integrative curricular, co-curricular and experiential pathways that progressively develop proficiencies?" (AAC&U, 2015b, p. 17).

At the program level, chronological coherence of courses and educational experiences is essential to develop students' achievement levels over time. Designed to prepare students to demonstrate the 186 program-level outcomes established by its specialized accreditor, the Accreditation Council for Occupational Therapy Education (ACOTE), the Occupational Therapy (OT) Department at Salem State University must know how well students are progressing toward achieving each of those outcomes. At the same time the department must remain knowledgeable about and responsive to the university's demographic diversity to enable students to achieve those outcomes equitably. Thus, the OT Department includes in its assessment plan a systematic and ongoing evaluation of its curricular coherence. This evaluation leads to timely and efficient response to data collected to promote students' development of both short-term and long-term professional knowledge and skills. To that end, faculty continuously evaluate their program based on numerous data sources and act on what they learn at the end of each semester. Included in those sources are course-based assessment results, students' evaluations of field-based experiences, test results, student self-surveys, fieldwork evaluations, graduate and employer surveys, and capstone course assignments. Jeramie Silveira, graduate coordinator in occupational therapy and faculty assessment fellow at Salem State University, identifies when and how faculty use these data: "The Occupational Therapy Assessment Committee compiles these data into reports for end-of semester faculty assessment meetings. These data are then used to make necessary modifications to the curriculum design, content, scope, and sequencing of courses to ensure a quality education program for its students" (personal communication, Occupational Therapy Program: Academic Year Assessment Timetable Salem State University, February 28, 2015; see the actual timetable in chapter 4, pp. 108–109).

Commitment 4: Alignment of Courses, Educational Experiences, and Assignments With Outcomes and Standards and Criteria of Judgment

Alignment, the fourth learner-centered commitment, involves educators designing their courses, modules, educational experiences, and assignments backward within the context of institution- and program-level outcomes and agreed-upon scoring rubrics or other metrics. The resulting coherence ensures that students have multiple and diverse opportunities to learn and practice agreed-upon general education and program-level outcomes across their degree pathway at more complex levels. If students do not see how the parts of these components of their education work together or contribute to general education- and program-level outcomes, they are likely to view their education as a process of traveling through silos, some of which may seem irrelevant to them. In fact, they may view certain courses or experiences solely as a means to amass credits and hours toward fulfilling degree requirements. The overarching alignment questions for educators are the following:

- How intentionally are courses, educational experiences, and assignments designed along students' pathways to advance students to attain high-quality degree- and program-level outcomes?
- What specific strategies, pedagogies, or contexts for learning in each course or educational experience enable students to progress toward attaining high-quality degree- and program-level outcomes?

Course and educational experience design requires identifying the pedagogies, educational practices, progression, and contexts for learning, such as peer-to-peer learning online, that foster and engage all students' achievement of targeted outcomes. Kuh (2008) identified a set of high-impact practices that have received national attention for their ability to engage all students. They include: first-year experiences and seminars, common intellectual experiences, learning communities, writing-intensive courses, collaborative assignments and projects, diversity/global learning, undergraduate research, service-learning, community-based learning, internships, and capstone courses and projects. These high-impact practices' contributions to underserved students' learning and success are documented in Finley and McNair's (2013) research, in which the authors conclude that positioning students to experience the relevance, transferability, and usefulness of what they are learning and have learned accounts for their learning gains. Yet, according to Kuh (2008), on many campuses, "Students from certain historically underserved groups are less likely to participate in some high-impact educational practices" (pp. 16–17). If historically underrepresented students, including those studying online, do not participate in these practices then determining how those students can be involved in high-impact experiences is immediately significant in the shared commitment to close achievement and degree completion gaps. Betts (2008), for example, identifies the range of possibilities for including high-impact practices in online programs.

Assignments that align not only with specified outcomes and scoring rubrics or other metrics but also with course or education experience sequencing contribute to students' awareness of their progress toward achieving course-level expectations as well as exit-level general education or major program expectations. Sequenced assignments, together with feedback to students and opportunities for them to reflect on their learning, help students learn about their patterns of strength and weakness as they prepare for a culminating assignment. On a larger scale, well-sequenced assignments across the general education program and major programs of study broaden and deepen students' understanding of the relevance and application of outcomes in diverse contexts other than the ones in which they initially learned them.

Recognition of the importance of assignment design and its alignment with outcomes and scoring rubrics has been identified in several large-scale projects. Among its GEM guideline questions AAC&U (2015b) asks, "Do faculty and staff work intentionally and collaboratively on the design of assignments that effectively help students practice, develop, and demonstrate cross-cutting proficiencies that the institution has articulated both for the degree and for general education?" (AAC&U, 2015b, p. 14). Faculty and administrator scorers in the two multi-institution large-scale pilot projects, Advancing a Massachusetts Culture of Assessment (AMCOA) and the MSC (see pp. 33–35), identified the importance of aligning assignment design with agreed-upon scoring rubrics used to assess students' achievement of specific general education outcomes. Assignments that were not aligned with the attributes and performance levels of a VALUE rubric or that were loosely or partially tethered to them often accounted for students' low performance. That observation led to asking whether some students would have performed better if the assignment had been intentionally designed to align with a specific rubric. To help two-year students successfully transfer into higher-level courses in four-year institutions, the Quality Collaboratives (QC) projects described in chapter 2 (pp. 37–38) also focused on assignment design between two-year and four-year institutions. The importance of assignment design underlies the National Institute for Learning Outcomes Assessment's (NILOA's) commitment to host national rounds of collaboratively designed DQP assignments, known as charrettes (NILOA, n.d.a). Examples of assignments that align with DQP outcomes are also featured in NILOA's Assignment Library (NILOA, n.d.c). Among AAC&U's LEAP resources, "Integrating Signature Assignments into the Curriculum" and "Inspiring Design" provide links to principles and examples of signature assignments in the general education curriculum and in major programs that require students to demonstrate one or more key outcomes during their undergraduate studies (AAC&U, n.d.).

In the Transparency in Teaching and Learning in Higher Education Project, Mary-Ann Winkelmes (2015) argues for making teaching and learning explicit for students by way of assignments. In relation to clearly identified program and general education outcomes, assignments identify the task students are required to address, the purpose of the task, and the criteria that will be used to assess that task. These components help students understand the relevance of an assignment. This understanding is especially important for historically underserved students who may lack knowledge about what to expect at this stage of their education, familiarity with the demands of postsecondary education, or understanding of what an assignment is asking them to demonstrate (Winkelmes et al., 2015, p. 4).

Commitment 5: Faculty Collaboration With the Institution's Network of Experts

Further strengthening the learner-centered canvas that spans across an outcomes-based framework is the fifth learner-centered commitment: faculty collaboration with the institution's network of experts. An inclusive commitment to student success leverages the expertise and experiences of professionals who support or contribute to student success, such as those in

- student affairs and support services,
- academic affairs and support services,
- library and information resources,
- registrar's office,
- institutional research,
- student enrollment and management,
- professional development,

- assessment,
- online education and education technology, and
- instructional design.

Experts in education technology, for example, contribute to the learner-centered design of courses, programs, and educational experiences. They identify options for complementary ways to improve or advance students' learning, which is especially effective when students demonstrate different levels of ability or understanding in a course. Representing some of those alternatives are

- websites or digital platforms that provide students with alternative ways to apply and extend their learning in new contexts, such as in interactive simulations;
- self-paced modules, courses, or programs that build in access to online tutors or supplemental instruction (a feature built into courses in online degrees); and
- online programs that provide real-time technology-enabled assessment results to both faculty and students, keeping them continuously informed of students' progress and challenges (see also Appendix 5).

Experts in professional development are knowledgeable about research on learning, the ways in which students learn and retain that learning, and the practices that engage students, such as the high-impact practices identified on pages 68 to 69 in this volume. Professional development experts are important contributors to the design or redesign of courses, syllabi, and education experiences that follow the principles of coherence and alignment.

Directors of writing centers, tutoring centers, and other learning support centers are individuals who learn firsthand about and respond immediately to students' academic needs. Many of these experts are often, and unfortunately, viewed as marginal contributors to student learning; yet the constant in their lives is addressing students' challenges in real time all the time. Typically, for example, faculty send students to support services. What if faculty could learn more about what these experts see in student work and how they address the range of issues that stump students? Or, how might faculty wrap some of those strategies around their face-to-face or online courses, especially high-risk courses?

At Auburn University, the director of the Miller Writing Center (MWC) works collaboratively with faculty across the institution to keep them informed about students' semester-by-semester writing challenges, as well as the sets of strategies the center uses to address those challenges, as illustrated in Case 3.2. Organized to support students' writing needs across all departments, the MWC recognizes the importance of responding on time to students' needs. Along with keeping semester-by-semester records of student demand, the MWC provides reports based on student demographics. In addition, the MWC can provide more substantive data from the work they do with students, as illustrated in its reports to the university's libraries. These kinds of data deepen faculty and other professionals' understanding of the ongoing writing challenges students face.

CASE 3.2.
The Miller Writing Center at Auburn University: Semester Monitoring of Statistics to Respond On-Time

The Miller Writing Center (MWC) at Auburn University is a cross-disciplinary writing center that serves students from all departments. We hire undergraduate and graduate consultants from all disciplines, and we partner with different departments and units to maintain multiple locations across campus to be accessible to as many students as possible. To ensure that we are meeting student needs at these locations, we regularly calculate location-specific usages during the semester and adjust staffing as necessary.

Usage statistics are the lifeblood of a writing center. As Schendel and Macauley (2012) say succinctly, "In writing centers, we are used to counting things" (p. xvi). How many students come to the MWC, when and how often they come, and their demographic range all define how writing centers are serving student needs. This emphasis on usage data rightly troubles writing center directors (WCDs), and much work is being done to move beyond tallying users and appointments to asking richer and more substantive questions about the work of writing centers as part of institutional support for student learning. For example, the MWC is collaborating with the Auburn Libraries, using data from the MWC system about student perceptions of scholarly research to develop more effective support for student writers at both the library reference desk and the writing center. But numbers still matter, particularly when arguing for budgetary resources to maintain or increase staffing.

WCOnline, a web-based scheduling system designed specifically for writing center use, reflects this emphasis on capturing usage data. The system allows the WCD to set up multiple schedules, customize enrollment questions about all users in the system, and run reports that break down statistics on both users and appointments across multiple schedules.

All user and appointment data can also be downloaded into Excel and be processed in more sophisticated ways. But the easiest and quickest data can be gathered from system utilization reports, which calculate the percentage of time used for appointments relative to the time offered on the schedule.

At the MWC we track this usage on a weekly basis to assess if locations are being overstressed. Writing center practice generally defines *maximum usage* as 80% across a semester. Student demand, however, varies depending on the timing of writing assignments; thus, usage will vary. If usage is consistently over 80%, students are likely turned away. Generally, usage assessment leads to changes made between semesters; in fall 2012, the usage at the main location in the Ralph B. Draughn (RBD) Library was over 80%, and other assessments showed that usage was peaking between 3:00 p.m. and 6:00 pm. As a result in spring 2013, an additional consultant was added to the schedule during those hours. This adjustment lowered usage at this location to 72%, taking pressure off the consultants and ensuring students were likely able to make appointments when they needed.

Early in fall 2014, we saw that the usage in RBD had moved back above 80%. We heard anecdotally from our front-desk staff at that location that students were attempting to make appointments, but when directed to other locations, they were not willing to cross campus. We made the decision to move some of the staff from other locations mid-semester to respond to student demand. In the following spring, we raised staffing for all hours at the RBD location to three consultants.

The ability to respond mid-semester has its limits; in the fall 2015 semester we once again faced usage over 80% at our RBD location, but our other locations were also showing increased usage, so reallocating resources was more difficult. We were able to justify a budget increase to add consultants to the schedule for the last two weeks of the semester, as well as increase staffing for spring 2016. As demonstrated by this example, monitoring usage data throughout the term allows us to make decisions that address both immediate and long-term student needs.

Note. Contributed by James C. W. Truman, assistant director, Office of University Writing, Auburn University. Used with permission.

Figure 3.1 represents the interdependency among core learner-centered commitments when an institution and its programs focus on students' equitable success. From left to right, the figure displays how the backward design of course or experience elements and assignments that assess students' learning are rooted in agreed-upon outcomes and scoring rubrics or other metrics that align with those outcomes.

Figure 3.1. Backward design of curricula and cocurricular programs to advance students to achieve high-quality outcomes.

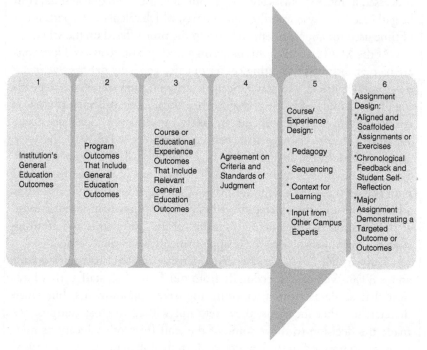

- Blocks 1, 2, and 3 represent coherence across the curriculum and cocurriculum. General education outcomes are addressed not only in an institution's general education program but also in students' major programs of study and educational experiences offered across the institution, such as in the cocurriculum. Multiple and diverse opportunities for students to practice and receive feedback on their achievement levels advance them to high-level achievement of degree- and program-level outcomes.
- Block 4 identifies the sequential importance of reaching agreement on sets of criteria and standards of judgment, such as the VALUE rubrics, that align with agreed-upon outcomes and specify shared expectations for students' high-quality achievement of those outcomes.
- Block 5 represents the alignment of course and educational experience components with agreed-upon outcomes and scoring rubrics or other metrics. This commitment helps students understand what, how, and how well they are learning in an individual course or experience as well as across their undergraduate studies. In this design phase, individuals from an institution's network of experts, such as instructional designers or librarians, contribute to course or experience design options.

- Block 6 identifies the importance of intentionally developing building block assignments and exercises in courses and experiences that
align with (a) agreed-upon outcomes and scoring rubrics and (b) the
progression of a course or experience that leads students to develop
a major or culminating work—exit-level assessment evidence of
students' performance levels.

Gaps in Learner-Centered Commitments: A Case Study

Because these learner-centered commitments are interdependent, focusing
on one to examine current assessment commitment often triggers deeper
inquiry into the others. Such was the case at Tidewater Community College
(TCC), a large, multicampus community college located in Virginia with
an annual enrollment of nearly 46,000. The catalyst for reforming its existing assessment commitment occurred when the college peeled back layers
of its assessment process after the results of a general education pilot project
were reviewed. To launch the pilot, there was agreement about the language
of VALUE rubrics and some internally developed rubrics to score students'
achievement of eight general education outcomes. The results of the pilot
project, however, revealed gaps in alignment, coherence, and a shared commitment to all students' success. Of importance in addressing these gaps is
how the institution relied on others across the institution, such as faculty
developers and the institution's Instruction Committee, and addressed policy
and procedures that have also now contributed to developing a shared commitment to students' learning, as described in Case 3.3.

CASE 3.3.
Tidewater Community College: Closing the Loop—Pedagogy, Curriculum, and Policy and Procedure Reform

This case describes how results of the collection and scoring of student work
identified gaps in the college's learner-centered commitments. To close
those gaps, the college acted on multiple fronts to address pedagogy and
assignments, curriculum reform, and institutional policies and procedures.

Pedagogy

Through the collection and scoring of student work products, it was clear
that faculty were not requiring course assignments and activities that

comprehensively supported or assessed student learning in the general education competency areas. Thus, the college's chief focus in facilitating student learning in the competencies has been on the professional development of faculty to better educate them about the general education assessment plan and to assist them in developing course assignments and activities reflective of the competencies. Examples include

- developing an online resource (General Education Assessment Resource System [GEARS]) by the Instruction Committee for faculty that provides samples of faculty-developed assignments that fully support student achievement in the competencies;
- devoting four Learning Institutes, the college's annual and premier faculty professional development event, to general education assessment related topics; and
- developing interdisciplinary and discipline-specific workshops focused on creating assignments that address the student learning outcomes.

Curriculum

Curriculum reform is under way as a result of the pilot. At least annually, faculty review the general education outcomes identified on course outlines and make adjustments as necessary. Unlike most other colleges involved in general education assessment, TCC requires each course, including career and technical offerings, to support at least one general education competency. Further, through a course-mapping process, the college identified programs that do not support all competencies through plan-specific requirements and collaborated with applicable faculty to address shortcomings.

Policy and Procedure

Pilot findings prompted the college to create policies and procedures to support the assessment plan. A small percentage of the faculty did not seem entirely supportive of the college's assessment efforts, and if their participation was expected as part of their performance evaluation, they wanted it documented. Hence, an academic standards policy was developed and implemented that describes the role and responsibilities of faculty and academic leaders in general education assessment. Another example of policy and procedure changes was the creation of a general education course selection procedure that requires courses serving as general education courses to wholly support a minimum of one general education competency.

Note. Contributed by Kellie Sorey, associate vice president for academics, Academic Affairs, Tidewater Community College. Used with permission.

As the TCC case study illustrates, gaps in an institution's set of learner-centered commitments erode the possibility of identifying and immediately addressing students' equitable progress toward achieving a high-quality degree. Altogether, the interdependent commitments described in this chapter weave the canvas that supports the principles of a real-time assessment process described in chapter 4.

4

GUIDING PRINCIPLES OF REAL-TIME STUDENT ASSESSMENT AT THE INSTITUTION AND PROGRAM LEVELS

R eal-time student assessment at the institution and program levels is sustained by a continuous inclusive and collaborative commitment to students' equitable attainment of a high-quality degree. Achieving that commitment requires (a) semester-by-semester reporting of assessment results documenting currently enrolled students' levels of achieving agreed-upon general education and major program outcomes, (b) interrogating underperformance patterns documented in assessment results when they occur and as they persist, and (c) nimbly developing on-time and longer-term interventions to improve students' learning continuously. Complementing other institutional efforts targeted to keep students on track to attain a degree—such as streamlining degree and program pathways, providing timely support services, or immediately identifying students who are missing classes—real-time assessment is a nonstop longitudinal commitment to students' academic success. To contribute to the integrity of this campus commitment, student data need to be accessible continuously to flag those who are facing or who continue to face challenges and to trigger immediate as well as longer-term interventions.

Developing real-time interventions or practices to address currently enrolled students' patterns of underperformance contributes to improving students' time to degree and measurably closing achievement and graduation gaps, particularly for those students identified in chapter 1. Close monitoring of students' achievement levels also becomes an institution's continuous means to target and address students' well-documented, persistent patterns of underperformance, such as in quantitative reasoning and problem-solving. These long-standing patterns are identified, for example, in Arum and Roksa's (2011) *Academically Adrift: Limited Learning on College Campuses* and research findings on the longitudinal Wabash National Study of Liberal Arts Education, 2006–2012 (Center of Inquiry in the Liberal Arts at Wabash College, n.d.). Reporting real-time assessment results at institution and program levels keeps internal stakeholders on the front line of students' progress. Results reported based on agreed-upon scoring rubrics or other metrics document patterns of continuous improved performance as well as patterns of stalled or persistent underperformance.

Chapter 3 identified the conditions for success that support real-time student assessment at the institution and program levels. Upon that foundation, in this chapter I

- identify the six principles of real-time student assessment,
- illustrate how campuses have operationalized or are operationalizing these principles to advance currently enrolled students to degree completion, and
- justify the relevance of real-time assessment for our currently enrolled students compared with more common point-in-time or cyclical assessment approaches that focus primarily on the work of students who have persisted.

Six Guiding Principles of Real-Time Student Assessment

Key to a continuous commitment to students' equitable academic progress toward achieving a high-quality degree is developing a real-time reporting system that enables internal stakeholders to see continuously how undergraduates are progressing. Real-time results fuel nimble actions to address patterns of underperformance when they occur and as they persist. Through this close gauging of and responding to students' academic progress, faculty and other contributors to student learning remain collaboratively focused on currently enrolled students' short- and long-term success, represented in the following two questions:

1. How well prepared are all students at the end of my course or education experience for the academic demands and expectations that lie ahead of them?

2. How well prepared are all students at the end of my course or education experience to continue to progress toward attaining high-quality exit-level institution- and program-level outcomes?

Thus, a real-time assessment commitment extends across students' undergraduate studies from point of matriculation, transfer, or reentry into a college or university to point of graduation. It values what matters most to faculty and other education professionals: individual student performance in their courses or educational experiences. Closing time gaps between more common institution- and program-level assessment approaches that occur only at points in time along students' undergraduate pathways, real-time assessment identifies the granular, context-based challenges that students face semester-by-semester or term-by-term. Posted end-of-course and educational experience assessment results formatively document how well all students—not a sample of students—are progressing toward achieving high-quality institution- and program-level outcomes. Sustained awareness of students' academic challenges, such as in critical thinking or writing, triggers developing on-time—and over time—interventions or practices to improve and thus advance currently enrolled students to achieve at higher levels. Figure 4.1 represents the movement of end-of-semester course- or experience-based assessment results into the wider contexts of each program and the institution, focused on all students' achievement of the program's or institution's

Figure 4.1. Movement of assessment results to develop a shared commitment to students' equitable progress.

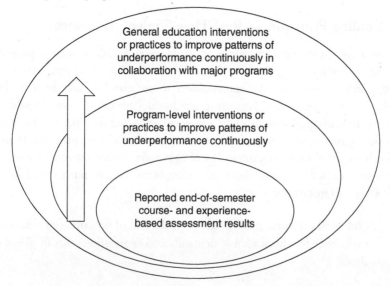

General education interventions or practices to improve patterns of underperformance continuously in collaboration with major programs

Program-level interventions or practices to improve patterns of underperformance continuously

Reported end-of-semester course- and experience-based assessment results general education outcomes. That movement engages others in interrogating results and identifying strategies to improve student learning continuously.

As the following six guiding principles of real-time student assessment indicate, disseminating assessment results continuously not only informs internal stakeholders, but also draws them into a shared commitment to improve students' underperformance patterns along their undergraduate studies.

Guiding Principle 1: Internally Driven and Motivated

An institution's mission or leadership, or both, instills a shared commitment to students' equitable success as the internal driver of real-time student assessment and other measures of student progress that identify immediate or potential challenges to their success. Some institutions' mission statements are the internal drivers of real-time student assessment. For example, the primary objective in Guttman Community College's mission statement (see Case 4.1, later in this chapter) is "to increase the number of students, especially those not effectively served in higher education, to persist in their programs of study and attain a degree in a timely manner" (guttman.cuny.edu/about/mission-vision-goals-outcomes). Carlow University's ethical commitment to real-time student assessment (Case 4.2, later in this chapter) is internally driven by the institution's mission, rooted in Mercy Catholic social justice tradition. Without an academic gauge of students' levels of achievement along their undergraduate pathway and the timely development of interventions or practices to address patterns of underperformance, disparities in achievement and completion rates across our student demographics remain.

In some cases, however, moving faculty and other contributors to student learning toward a shared commitment to all students' success may meet resistance. Faculty may say outright that meeting annual or longer-term graduation goals will result in having to pass more students or water down expectations for their performance; yet working within a shared outcomes-based framework and aligned scoring rubrics or other metrics raises the bar for all students. At the same time, advancing students to demonstrate higher achievement levels becomes a shared responsibility along the trajectory of students' pathways, not the commitment of some. Thus, semester-by-semester course- and experience-based assessment results document students' levels of performance as well as the continued need to address patterns of underperformance. Others across an institution may take a fatalistic view of measurably closing achievement or degree completion rates. Some may respond by blaming students for not trying hard enough or for not being prepared for college, thus contributing to persistent low retention or high failure rates. Still others may say they are doing all they can right now, but their efforts are not cutting into existing gaps; thus, gaps are inevitable. Accepting disparities as "givens" inhibits efforts to learn about the causes of chronological and often persistent academic challenges students face and then to develop practices that help them overcome those challenges. Gaps, according to Joseph Yeado, policy analyst at the Education Trust, are not inevitable. Based on U.S. Department of Education graduation rates in postsecondary institutions from 2009 to 2011, the analyst identified institutions with the same student profiles and admission requirements that have successfully closed or are closing gaps between White students and Black and Hispanic students. Accounting for these high-performing institutions' success is a shared and highly intentional commitment to improve graduation rates by developing proven practices and policies across these institutions that close achievement and graduation gaps. According to Yeado (2013), "A groundswell of committed institutions could accelerate national graduation rates to new and higher levels for all students and help remedy racial and socioeconomic inequities in education and beyond" (p. 4).

Guiding Principle 2: Inclusive of Internal Stakeholders

An inclusive commitment to real-time student assessment stretches across an institution and engages internal stakeholders at multiple levels and for various purposes—from institution or system leaders to administrators; academic leaders; full- and part-time faculty; the institution's network of experts who contribute to or support student learning, identified in chapter 3 (pp. 70–71); and currently enrolled students. All these stakeholders contribute to this assessment approach.

For chancellors, presidents, senior administrative leaders, and academic leaders, continuous reporting of real-time assessment results documents how students are progressing academically—a picture that may not yet be available on many campuses. Fresh data reported semester-by-semester or at other short intervals in an academic year, such as at midsemester, document students' actual progress against agreed-upon scoring rubrics or other metrics. These data trigger the need to develop immediate as well as short- and long-term interventions that may require financial support, additional resources, or reallocation of resources. For example, an institutional leader may decide to direct resources to address persistent patterns of underperformance that occur in high-risk courses such as early credit-bearing mathematics courses, as described in chapter 3 (pp. 59–60). As a result, an institution's chief financial officer becomes another involved internal stakeholder.

Seeing documented achievement gaps represented in real-time assessment data prompts deans, chairs, and provosts to focus faculty attention on them by developing interventions or practices to close those gaps for currently enrolled students. Failing to include and draw on the knowledge and experiences of part-time faculty limits the pool of possible interventions that may be implemented to address the gaps that exist across an institution's student demographics. In fact, in some cases, part-time faculty may teach higher percentages of traditionally underrepresented students than full-time faculty, such as first-generation, working, or part-time students. A shared commitment to students' success in real-time student assessment also purposefully includes individuals from the institution's network of experts (see chapter 3, pp. 70–71). Including these professionals in real-time student assessment builds a commitment that benefits from different areas of expertise. Under this second principle, everyone who teaches or contributes to student learning matters, because students' equitable progress matters.

Deepening interrogation of real-time assessment results are the words of students themselves, the largest group of internal stakeholders. Because real-time assessment focuses on students' equitable progress toward degree completion, including students' perspectives on their learning and the challenges they face is essential to an institution's shared commitment to currently enrolled students' success. Students' formative or end-of-course or education experience feedback needs to be folded into a full interrogation of assessment results and identification of actions to improve student learning. One possibility for gathering students' course-based feedback is the online survey titled Student Assessment of Their Learning Gains (www.salgsite.org). This survey asks students to identify how well they believe they achieved or did not achieve course or educational experience outcomes and why. Another possibility is to use the practice of small-group instructional diagnosis as students are taking a course (Ferris State University, n.d.). An invited colleague interviews students in a course or educational experience about challenges they are facing. Those results go directly to the individual teaching a course or offering an education experience to ensure that student responses are addressed in a timely manner. Reading or hearing about how students experience their learning also contributes to the process of identifying practices to improve students' patterns of underperformance in the next offering of that course and in subsequent courses as well.

Guiding Principle 3: Bolstered by Collaboration That Harnesses Others' Expertise and Practices

Collaboration among program faculty, among faculty who contribute to students' general education outcomes, and between faculty and the institution's network of experts harnesses others' expertise and practices in an on-the-ground commitment to improve currently enrolled students' learning. Drawing on others' expertise and practices expands the processes of interrogating real-time assessment results and identifying practices or strategies that help students improve their achievement levels.

At the level of students' major programs, full- and part-time faculty and others who contribute to student learning, such as field supervisors or community service coordinators, individually report assessment results semester-by-semester. Results are reported based on scoring student work that demonstrates agreed-upon disciplinary, field-specific, or professional outcomes and integrated general education outcomes. Agreed-upon scoring rubrics provide a consistent way to report and gauge students' achievement of those outcomes. Individuals who address the same outcome(s) in their courses or educational experiences identify patterns of underperformance and ways in which they can individually as well as collaboratively and chronologically improve those patterns for currently enrolled students. Specific interventions to improve underperformance patterns reported at the end of a semester are put in place for the next scheduled offering of those courses or experiences. Continuing to address those patterns of underperformance in students' remaining courses, however, requires collaboration among colleagues to contribute to students' equitable success. Other interventions or strategies need to be put in place in subsequent courses to address underperformance patterns continuously for currently enrolled students, such as weak abilities to synthesize or analyze. Collaboration among faculty also occurs in another context: interrogating general education assessment results. This collaboration brings together not only those who teach general education courses but also those who address general education outcomes in students' major programs of study. This broad-based collaboration aims to continue to monitor students' achievement of general education outcomes beyond the general education curriculum in a commitment to ensure that students are equitably prepared with the necessary intellectual skills, such as written communication, teamwork, integrative learning, and critical thinking. At both the general education and program levels, reporting course- or educational experience–based assessment results leads to highly contextualized interrogation of results and specific real-time actions that reach across students' undergraduate studies.

Equal to their contributions to the design of courses, programs, and educational experiences discussed in the previous chapter are those that professionals in the institution's network of experts make to interrogate assessment results or expand the pool of on-time practices that faculty can use to improve student learning. Many professionals from an institution's expert network can report on the patterns of student behavior they either see themselves or hear about from students. That is, they are eyewitnesses to how students perform or what they struggle to accomplish. Among such individuals are those in support centers, advising centers, and the library. Drawing on what these individuals experience firsthand sensitizes faculty to the real-time obstacles that impede students' progress and time to degree. That deepened understanding pulls faculty more directly into addressing retention, achievement, and graduation rates, issues that, according to Tinto (2012), "rarely involve the faculty, and as a result rarely impact classroom practices" (pp. 1–2). For example, a counselor may hear about first-generation students' confusion about what an assignment is asking them to demonstrate or how they should tackle it.

Individuals from the institution's expert network are also sources of student data. Specifically, the registrar can report dismissal, withdrawal, fail (DWF) rates in real time. Student affairs professionals who also assess general education outcomes can share their results with faculty to develop shared practices designed to improve patterns of underperformance or to identify differences in cocurricular and academic results and why those occur. The institution's expert network also serves as a storehouse of additional educational practices that can expand the pool of interventions or strategies that faculty can draw upon to address patterns of underperformance. Contributing to that storehouse, for example, are people in academic support centers who address student obstacles daily or those in education technology who can identify the range of options in education technology to address patterns of student underperformance. These options can be integrated into or surround courses and educational experiences.

Other campus experts, such as institutional researchers, student information system directors, and enrollment management and retention directors, also have access to student data that can complement real-time discussions. These individuals report on patterns of students' performance, behaviors, perceptions of their learning gains, and satisfaction with institution- and program-level practices and services. For many institutions, access to these kinds of data in real time is limited because different systems are used to collect, analyze, and report data; therefore, it is difficult to coordinate reporting of those results with assessment results. Being able to house student data in one system is, of course, ideal—an investment that contributes to a real-time assessment process and on-time responses. Not surprisingly then, among the key developments that significantly contributed to the eight institutions' success in measurably closing achievement gaps (see this volume, pp. 59–60) is a "very sophisticated student success data management system" that includes the capacity to monitor students' progress and alert faculty and advisors when students are unable to meet expectations (Yeado, Haycock, Johnstone, & Chaplot, 2014, p. 2). Authors also report that none of those institutions had such a system before they became involved in their comprehensive institutional commitment to improve retention and graduation rates. To contribute to the integrity of this campus commitment, student data need to be accessible to (a) flag those who are facing or who continue to face challenges and (b) trigger immediate as well as longer-term interventions. Absent a single data system, key to real-time assessment is identifying the kinds of data that are currently available and relevant to learn about in the processes of interrogating students' patterns of performance, and then identifying on-time interventions to improve underperformance patterns.

Chapter 5 identifies some of the ways in which technology contributes to time gaps that may currently exist between when student data are collected and when those data are analyzed and accessible to faculty and others for on-time action.

Guiding Principle 4: Anchored in Continuous Reporting and Interrogation of Assessment Results

A shared commitment to students' equitable long-term success is anchored in continuously reporting assessment results to track students' general education and major program outcomes. Based on agreed-upon general education and program-level outcomes and aligned scoring rubrics or other metrics, real-time assessment results are displayed on two dashboards: program-level dashboards and an institution-level dashboard. Assessment results are reported and displayed beginning at the point of students' matriculation, transfer, or reentry and extending to graduation. These dashboards enable presidents, provosts, deans, and chairs to gauge closely students' equitable progress toward achieving high-quality institution-level outcomes—specifically, general education outcomes and major program outcomes. Seeing assessment results displayed on dashboards fuels the need to develop on-time educational practices that address patterns of underperformance when they occur and as they persist. Hoping someone else will intervene to address underperformance patterns in a future course or courses is not a strategy. Developing a shared commitment to improve students' underperformance patterns continuously is a strategy. Posting end-of-semester granular course- and educational experience–based results facilitates relevant contextualized interrogation that leads to agreed-upon timely actions to improve those results. In contrast to scheduled assessment approaches that occur over stretches of time and often are time-consuming to complete, real-time assessment closes those time gaps to maintain a commitment to all students' progress. Further, this approach to assessment leads to specific context-based actions to improve currently enrolled students' learning in the short and long term. It stands in contrast with assessment approaches that separate faculty in time from students' specific learning contexts and, therefore, distance them from being able to identify specific interventions or practices.

(Fine-grained dashboard reporting options are identified in chapter 5, enabling internal stakeholders to visualize and interact with reported assessment data.)

Program-Level Dashboard

A program-level dashboard monitors students' equitable achievement of major program outcomes and general education outcomes addressed within the context of majors, such as quantitative reasoning, writing, speaking, teamwork, and problem-solving. Collaborative interrogation of posted assessment results for each course or educational experience and identification of short- and long-term practices to improve patterns of underperformance begin as soon as possible after real-time student assessment results are posted. Typically, program-level outcome assessment results are displayed at the end of each semester or term or at other short intervals of time in an academic year to monitor students' progress continuously. In addition to end-of-semester dashboard postings, many programs also schedule other times to assess their students' learning. For example, some preassess declared majors' level of preparation. These results document patterns of weakness that program-level faculty need to attend to, beginning with students' first course. Some programs may also establish semester check-in times to identify and address challenges that students face that jeopardize their ability to succeed in a specific course as well as in future courses. Immediate interventions need to be developed to keep these students on track. Waiting until the end of a semester or term to identify and address patterns of underperformance may be too late to take actions that help students overcome their academic challenges.

With end-of-semester dashboard-displayed assessment results available to all members of a program—provosts, deans, chairs, and so on—a program's assessment liaison or an assessment director should schedule an end-of-semester meeting. These regularly scheduled meetings rely on individuals' scoring results as formative evidence of students' equitable progress toward achieving high-quality program-level outcomes. In the company of colleagues and others who contribute to or support student learning, individuals reflect on and discuss their course- or experience-based results, including students' feedback if it is available. To remain focused on students' progress, the goals of these regularly scheduled meetings are to

- identify and explore the root causes of course- or educational experience–based patterns of underperformance, such as students' inabilities to apply learning or synthesize;

- identify practices or interventions to implement in the next offering of that course to address patterns of underperformance or to implement immediately if results are reported during a semester;
- discuss practices or interventions that other faculty and contributors to student learning will use in subsequent courses or education experiences to address those patterns continuously for currently enrolled students.

In a shared commitment to students' equitable progress toward attaining high-quality program-level outcomes, colleagues and others who support and contribute to student learning contribute to these goals (refer also to principles 2 and 3 in this chapter). Without an inclusive commitment to students' success, individuals live in silos outside of the context of others' expectations for student progress, including agreed-upon final achievement levels. Interrogating assessment results with colleagues and others who contribute to or support student learning maintains a shared focus on students' realistic progress and a shared commitment to addressing patterns of underperformance when they occur or as they persist.

Semester-by-semester program-level dashboards document the efficacy of implemented actions or identify the need for other or continuous interventions if underperformance patterns persist. Many underperformance patterns require sustained longitudinal attention, not periodic attention. In this case the provost or vice president of academic affairs, together with the institution's assessment director, schedules time with a program's academic leader to determine how faculty will handle a particular underperformance pattern. Sustained patterns of underperformance challenge the assumption that all students transfer previous learning or even improved patterns of performance into a subsequent or higher-level course or educational experience. Students' enduring learning develops over time, usually as a result of diverse and multiple opportunities to apply, practice, and receive feedback on that learning. Continuously seeing students' progress reported on a dashboard sharpens faculty members' and others' focus on students' equitable progress.

Institution-Level Dashboard

An institution-level dashboard monitors students' equitable achievement of the institution's general education outcomes based on semester-by-semester assessment results reported from the following sources: (a) courses and related educational experiences in the institutions' formal general education curriculum and (b) major program courses and related educational experiences that advance students' performance of general education outcomes. These assessment results identify patterns of underperformance that need to be addressed in the short and long term to close currently enrolled students' gaps in achieving high-quality liberal education outcomes. Similar to the inclusive and collaborative end-of-semester program-level exchanges that take place are annual convenings that draw together individuals across an institution who contribute to students' achievement of general education outcomes. At this level of inquiry and action, communities of individuals who address a specific general education outcome are formed. These communities include

- the director of the institution's general education program of study;
- faculty who teach general education courses or offer related educational experiences;
- faculty in students' major programs of study who also contribute to advancing students' achievement of general education outcomes in their courses and educational experiences, such as intercultural knowledge and competence, writing, and speaking in business courses; and
- representatives from the institution's network of experts who deepen interrogation of assessment results and expand the pool of possible interventions or practices to improve learning.

An institution's assessment director, together with its director of general education, annually schedules these general education community convenings. Seasoned faculty and staff who have experience teaching general education courses or designing related educational experiences can effectively lead these convenings as well. Similar to end-of-semester program-level meetings focused on investigating assessment results and identifying actions to improve patterns of underperformance, annual institution-level convenings focus on the same processes. Assessment results for general education outcomes addressed in major programs of study are discussed in the presence of colleagues from other major programs in a commitment to students' equitable progress toward achieving those outcomes at high levels across the institution. These convenings respect the different contexts within which students continue to practice general education outcomes, such as writing. At the same time they become an occasion for colleagues from various major programs of study to learn about and draw from the strategies or interventions that other colleagues use to address persistent patterns of underperformance in student work demonstrating general education outcomes. The repertoire of strategies that unfolds benefits the larger community of those who contribute to students' general education learning. Altogether and in collaboration with professionals from the institution's network of experts, these annual convenings can forge a longitudinal commitment to improving students' abilities to achieve high-quality general education outcomes. Without this level of shared commitment, a focus on students' equitable progress toward achieving an institution's stated high-quality exit-level general education outcomes remains uneven or fades. How well students continue to progress and improve their general education outcomes is a responsibility of each major program together with an institution's general education program, documented in students' final or near-final coursework.

Figure 4.2 identifies the semester-by-semester assessment results that internal stakeholders have access to via program-level dashboards and the institution-level dashboard, which monitors students' progress toward achieving high-quality general education outcomes addressed in the general

Figure 4.2. Posting assessment results documenting students' achievement levels of program- and institution-level outcomes to gauge continuously students' equitable progress toward degree completion.

The Program-Level Dashboard

A program-level dashboard documents students' progress toward achieving high-quality major program outcomes.

Assessment results for students' achievement of general education outcomes addressed in students' major programs of study are also sent to the institution-level dashboard.

The Institution-Level Dashboard

The institution-level dashboard documents students' progress toward achieving high-quality general education outcomes developed in the institution's general education program of study and in students' major programs of study.

Posted program-level assessment results are interrogated as soon as possible to identify interventions or practices to improve currently enrolled students' learning. In some cases—to keep students on track—results are posted at a point in a semester, fueling immediate interventions. Short- and long-term interventions or practices address persistent patterns of underperformance.

Posted general education assessment results reported from the general education program of study and from major programs of study are interrogated annually to identify interventions or practices to improve currently enrolled students' learning. In some cases—to keep students on track—results are posted at a point in a semester, fueling immediate interventions. Short- and long-term interventions or practices address persistent patterns of underperformance.

education program and in students' major programs of study. These dash-boards document in real time students' achievement levels based on agreed-upon program and general education outcomes. Real-time postings on each of the dashboards fuel on-time interrogation of underperformance patterns reflected in students' authentic work. These context-specific interrogations lead, in turn, to specific actions to improve student learning in the short and long term. Chapter 5 (pp. 123–126) presents some of the various ways in which general education and program-level assessment results can be dis-played.

Guiding Principle 5: Responsive to Students' Needs in the Present Tense

Ensuring that currently enrolled students equitably progress toward attaining a high-quality degree requires nimble, targeted, and context-based interven-tions, strategies, and practices to close existing achievement and graduation gaps. To close those gaps measurably requires that institutions and their programs disaggregate assessment results based on student demographics. Monitoring and responding in real time to our diverse student populations' academic challenges or struggles is an essential component of this granu-lar assessment approach. Harris and Bensimon (2007) identified the serious consequences of institutions' failure to track minority students' progress and regularly address their patterns of underperformance:

> If the academic outcomes of minority students are not assessed regularly and treated as measurable evidence of institutional performance, we can expect inequalities in outcomes to remain structurally hidden and unattended to. We believe that collecting data on student outcomes disaggregated by race and reporting on them regularly should be a standard operating practice in colleges and universities. (p. 77)

Those dire consequences take on even broader significance now, as our insti-tutions experience the widening spectrum of student diversity described in chapter 1. However, it is not yet a pervasive institutional practice to disag-gregate assessment results based on student demographics. Key findings from the AAC&U's 2015 survey of 1,001 of its member institutions, representing all sectors of higher education, point up that demographic disaggregation of assessment results is not yet a high priority. Survey findings also include results of in-depth interviews with 14 administrators about their institutional priorities for tracking and advancing underserved students' success. Those who responded to the AAC&U survey stated they typically do "track stu-dents' achievement of learning" (AAC&U, 2016, p. 2); however, "few are disaggregating data by various student demographics (e.g., race/ethnicity, income levels or parental education levels)" (p. 6).

Further distancing an institution and its programs from the academic realities of its currently enrolled students are extended time gaps that commonly exist between scheduled institution- and program-level assessment periods, often timed to meet external mandates. These gaps represent missed opportunities to identify students who struggle, because the only students who are assessed during those points in time are those who are still in the system. Disparities in achievement across those time gaps are not addressed; they remain invisible, just as are the students who dropped out or failed in those time gaps. In addition, on many campuses, assessment cycles are often limited to one or a set of outcomes. Other equally important outcomes remain unaddressed until another cycle is initiated. These cycles may extend over long periods of time—from one to multiple years—before results are acted upon to improve student learning. Meanwhile, currently enrolled students may benefit little from interventions or new practices proposed at the end of those cycles. Even if some do, what about the other outcomes that students could have improved but that were not addressed during their undergraduate studies? In contrast to these delayed-response assessment approaches or wait-and-see approaches, real-time assessment requires living continuously with and acting on assessment results reported at the course and education experience levels. Results at these levels document how well students continue to retain, apply, and integrate general education and major program outcomes in different contexts and for a range of purposes.

Guiding Principle 6: Valued by the Institution

More than a service to the institution, real-time assessment reflects a shared and sustained commitment to all currently enrolled students' success. Institutionally valuing this work based on a college's or university's reward and recognition practices elevates the significance of this effort. One of the ways institutional leaders value this work is by acknowledging that it takes time. Explicitly designating a specific number of days in an academic year for assessment work to take place, such as program-level meeting days when patterns of underperformance are discussed and then acted upon, is one way to value this work. Dedicating necessary resources or support to carry out real-time assessment, such as technological support, represents another way institutional leaders value the commitment. In its promotion or tenure systems, an institution might, for example, value individuals' engagement in real-time assessment based on the following kinds of commitments: (a) developing innovations, strategies, or approaches to teaching and learning that help students overcome learning barriers; (b) disseminating and sustaining those developments; (c) taking effective teaching or learning strategies to scale to improve student learning in other or related courses or contexts; or (d) engaging in the scholarship of teaching and learning (SoTL).

Four Case Studies That Illustrate the Six Principles of Real-Time Student Assessment

Institutional cultures, structures, norms, and ways of behaving have direct bearing on how an institution or even its programs develop a commitment to real-time student assessment. For that reason the following four case studies illustrate different ways campuses have operationalized or are operationalizing the principles of real-time assessment. Cases 4.1 to 4.3 provide examples of institution-level real-time assessment—one at a graduate institution, illustrating that this process is also attainable at a higher degree level. Annotations in these case studies identify how each institution has integrated the six principles into the fabric of its culture. Case 4.4 describes the assessment timetable a program follows to assess all students continuously. All of these cases illustrate the importance of agreeing on outcomes-based frameworks to track students' equitable progress. Three of the four case studies identify how their assessment management systems or learning management systems contribute to their real-time assessment commitment (chapter 5 describes the advantages of these systems in more detail). Requiring students to maintain their coursework in ePortfolios—the same coursework that is the basis of reporting program- and institution-level assessment results—is discussed in three case studies. Thus, students are also held accountable continuously for their progress.

Case 4.1. Guttman Community College: Assessment as Catalyst and Keystone for Learning

Case 4.1 describes how a collaborative and real-time commitment to students' attainment of a degree is evolving at Guttman Community College. In this case, the college's mission—to prepare "those not effectively served in higher education"—drives a shared, internal commitment to each enrolled student's success. Also internally motivating this work is Guttman's president, who remains informed of students' needs and attends as many scheduled assessment days as possible. As the case details, focus on students' performance begins in the college's Summer Bridge program, initially providing valuable assessment data about the kinds of challenges students face. The program also initiated ePortfolios as a way to engage student learning. Recognizing that assessment is an ongoing commitment to its students, the institution builds 10 Assessment Days each year into the academic calendar. These days include engaging internal stakeholders across the college in assessment-related activities such as assessing and sharing assessment results, interpreting and acting on those results to improve currently enrolled students' learning in real time, and offering related professional development activities. Faculty and the campus's network of experts contribute to student learning, working together during those assessment days. At the college, the associate dean of assessment and technology is responsible for keeping the president apprised of the results of those days, many of which the president is able to attend.

CASE 4.1.
Guttman Community College:
Assessment as Catalyst and Keystone for Learning

Stella and Charles Guttman Community College, the newest community college in the City University of New York, welcomed its inaugural class of students in 2012. Our mission statement identifies our **Principle 1:** primary objective—"to increase the number of students, **Internally driven** especially those not effectively served in higher educa- **by its mission** tion, to persist in their programs of study and attain a degree in a timely manner." Our bold, innovative educational model (see Figure 4.1.1 at the end of this case) is designed to help urban community college students persist and graduate. Bringing together multiple high-impact practices (Kuh, 2008) such as first-year experience, learning communities, and experiential education at-scale, we hope to significantly increase student engagement, success, and graduation rates. Assessment of student learning and of our educational model is essential to our success. We strive to build a culture of learning for our students and for ourselves; assessment is the keystone of that learning culture. There are three focus areas of Guttman's assessment work: student learning, the educational model, and institutional effectiveness. Assessment in each of these areas is guided by the associate dean for assessment and technology and the director of the center for college effectiveness, who partner in their efforts to create a culture of learning and improvement across the institution.

Assessing Student Learning

Prior to the opening of the college, faculty and staff created the first iteration of our institutional student learning outcomes. Rebranded as the Guttman Learning Outcomes (GLOs) in 2013, these outcomes and corresponding rubrics were developed using the DQP, the LEAP ELOs, and AAC&U's VALUE rubrics. The GLOs encourage students to "aim high and provide them with a framework for their entire educational experience, connecting school, college, work and life" (guttman.cuny.edu/about/mission-vision-goals-outcomes/learning-outcomes). In its statement of learning outcomes for its diverse student body, Guttman identifies its institutional commitment to assessment as follows:

> Students will know from the time they enter Guttman Community College that they will be expected to demonstrate progress in achieving these outcomes. Institutional learning outcomes will be addressed at the course and program level. They will be based on integrative learning in and beyond the classroom and will be assessed via students' coursework as collected and presented in their ePortfolios. (guttman.cuny.edu/about/mission-vision-goals-outcomes/learning-outcomes)

Principle 3: Collaborative, including engaging students in documenting their progress toward achieving outcomes

The use of ePortfolios is essential to student learning itself and the assessment of student learning. Making learning visible, ePortfolios engage students, help them develop academic goals and plans, and enable them to see their own learning trajectory. For faculty and staff, ePortfolios ground assessment in authentic student work and student reflection. All students at the college create an ePortfolio during their Summer Bridge program. Bringing together curricular, cocurricular, and advising and planning experiences, students' ePortfolios serve as a space for learning, reflection, and planning throughout their time at Guttman.

In 2013, a group of faculty, staff, and administrators attended AAC&U's General Education Institute. While there, they developed a plan for assessment of student learning: a team of faculty and staff would assess each GLO over a three-year period. The design principles of inquiry, reflection, and integration guide each year of the GLO team's work. In addition, Guttman now has 10 Assessment Days built into its academic calendar. These days, which occur at the mid- and endpoints of our semesters, provide faculty and staff the time and space to assess student learning. Activities on these days include GLO team meetings,

Principle 6: Institutionally valued by building 10 Assessment Days into the academic calendar in recognition of needed time

assessment of student work via ePortfolios, reflection on   **Principle 4:**
assessment and survey data and assignment design workshops,   **Anchored in**
and other professional development activities. For example, at   **continuous**
  reporting
some of our most recent Assessment Days, faculty and staff   **and acting on**
assessed students' ePortfolios as part of the civic learning and   **assessment**
intellectual skills GLO assessment. Formative feedback from   **results**
that assessment led to an assignment design workshop where faculty worked
together to more directly connect the GLOs to their assignments. In addition,
we are developing a stronger ePortfolio structure to facilitate the assessment
process.

Assessing Guttman's Educational Model

Each major component of Guttman's educational model (i.e., Summer
Bridge, instructional teams, and academic support) is assessed. Working with
key faculty and staff, the associate dean and center director   **Principle 2:**
develop an assessment plan. Data are gathered, evaluated,   **Inclusive of**
and shared. Through a collaborative process with key faculty   **faculty, staff,**
  administrators,
and staff stakeholders, recommendations are generated and   **and students**
used to guide the integration of curricular and cocurricular
improvements. For example, the academic assessment plan   **Principle 3:**
for the Summer Bridge program includes a student survey,   **Collaborative**
faculty survey, and a review of student work in their ePortfolios. In our initial
assessment of the Summer Bridge program, student survey results indicated
that students were struggling with ePortfolios. The Summer   **Principle 5:**
Bridge Committee immediately developed activities across   **Responsive to**
the Summer Bridge curriculum to better integrate students'   **students' needs**
  in the present
use of ePortfolios. Students' use and understanding of ePort-   **tense**
folios have improved each year since that initial assessment.

    Our academic support network also uses multiple meth-   **Principle 2:**
ods of assessment. The peer mentor program and advise-   **Inclusive**
ment team of student success advocates and career strategists
rely on student surveys, faculty surveys, focus groups, ePort-   **Principle 5:**
  Responsive to
folio reflections, and sign-in logs as information about the   **students' needs**
use and usefulness of these services. This feedback contrib-   **in the present**
uted to refinement of peer mentors' responsibilities and   **tense**
advising events. These refinements were particularly important to ensure
high-quality attention to the college's increasing number of students.

    In addition to assessing the components of our model, each of our
five degree programs as well as the First-Year Experience program will

engage in a periodic program review (PPR) and self-study. Following the structure of the GLO Assessment plan, PPRs will take place over a three-year cycle, using the framework of inquiry, reflection, and integration to guide the work of the program review team. We are still in the formative stage of this work; in 2014 our two largest degree programs, liberal arts and sciences and business administration, began year one (inquiry) of the PPR process.

Assessing Institutional Effectiveness

The Systematic Approach for Guttman Effectiveness **Principle 3:** (SAGE) is a framework for institutional effectiveness and **Collaborative** continuous improvement. SAGE engages administrative areas across the college in reflection and direction, looking back at challenges and accomplishments and looking ahead at enhancing practices. Through SAGE, college staff members participate in a four-part process: (a) mapping plans, (b) identifying relevant assessment methods and data support, (c) linking practices and resources, and (d) analyzing results to identify strengths and areas for improvements. To promote the SAGE culture, the Center for College Effectiveness hosts professional development sessions and one-on-one consultations with college areas. In addition, during Assessment Days, staff have opportunities to coordinate efforts, provide feedback to each other, and showcase their SAGE plans. Overall, SAGE is a participatory, practical process in which participants are leaders and learners.

Assessment as Catalyst and Keystone

Through these three assessment areas—student learning, the educational model, and institutional effectiveness—we are working to cultivate a learning culture at Guttman. The 10 Assessment Days each year anchor assessment as a keystone of the college, engaging faculty and staff in a systematic and recursive inquiry, reflection, and integration process. While our work in many ways is still formative, as we begin to close the loop in our various assessments, faculty and staff are able to see the ways assessment serves as a catalyst for learning and improvement.

The president remains informed of developments **Principle 1:** from the 10 Assessment Days through periodic reports **Internally** from the associate dean for assessment and technology. In **motivated by the president** addition, he often attends these days when his schedule permits to remain aware of student needs.

Figure 4.1.1. Guttman Community College education model.

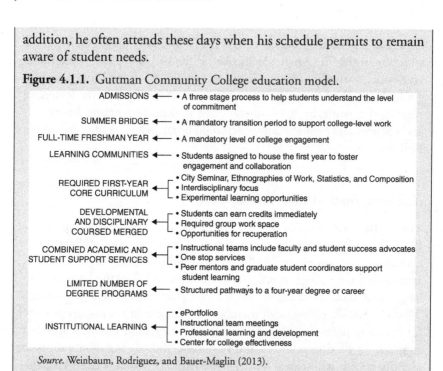

Source. Weinbaum, Rodriguez, and Bauer-Maglin (2013).

Note. Contributed by Laura M. Gambino, associate dean for assessment and technology, Guttman Community College. Used with permission.

Case 4.2. Carlow University: An Ethical Imperative

For Carlow University, the institution's shared commitment to real-time assessment is driven by its ethical mission-bound imperative to prepare each of its students. Half of its students are Pell recipients; 60% do not have a parent with a college degree. Real-time assessment is also internally motivated by senior leadership that has taken steps to present this commitment as an inclusive and collaborative one. Additionally, leadership remains involved in learning about students' progress semester-by-semester and recognizes that time and resources are necessary to enable educators to sustain a commitment to all currently enrolled students' success. Collaboratively agreed-upon outcomes-based frameworks for the university's general education program, the Compass Curriculum, and its major programs of study support the university's real-time semester-by-semester commitment. An additional integrative upper-level general education course again assesses students' general education outcomes to identify students, including transfer students, who need additional support to improve their general education achievement levels.

CASE 4.2.
Carlow University: An Ethical Imperative

To make learning outcomes assessment truly a part of its institutional fabric, Carlow University realized that the importance and meaningfulness of the assessment process could not be rooted solely in a mandate from a seemingly faraway, external organization such as an accreditor. In the Carlow ethos, the faculty, staff, and university community have a strong respect for and deep connection to the institution's mission, which is rooted in the Mercy Catholic social justice tradition and focuses on creating "a just and merciful world." With this in mind, Carlow has framed the implementation of learning assessment processes as an ethical imperative. Approximately half of Carlow's undergraduate students are Pell-eligible, and 60% do not have a parent with a college degree. This, combined with the rising costs of higher education, means that we must do everything in our power to ensure they receive the education—the learning outcomes—that they seek. We have an ethical, mission-grounded obligation to these students.

> Principle 1: Internally driven by the institution's ethical imperative to its student demographics

Considering this, the assessment process provides a means for us to reflect on, improve, and confidently understand the impact we have on the development of our students as we strive to empower them to excel as compassionate, responsible, and active participants in the creation of a just and merciful world. This message has served as a foundation for the successful development, growth, and momentum of Carlow's learning assessment processes. The president and provost have stressed this message, communicating it at university faculty assemblies, embedding it in the student handbook, and presenting it to faculty and staff as the rationale for their commitment to assessment. Ultimately, this campaign for mission-grounded learning assessment led to the establishment of strong assessment frameworks within the university's general education and disciplinary programs.

> Principle 1: Internally motivated by senior administrators

> Principle 2: Inclusive of faculty, staff, and institutional leadership

Assessing Student Learning Within the General Education Curriculum

In fall 2013 Carlow issued an institution-wide call for faculty, staff, and students to participate in the creation of a shared set of institutional learning outcomes that reflect the unique characteristics of a Carlow education.

A representative leadership team collected from the campus community definitions of and ideas and recommendations for learning outcomes. They refined this material via an iterative, open-feedback process and prepared a draft set of learning outcomes for review by the university community. The effort culminated in a daylong event organized by the provost; facilitated by the leadership team; and attended by over half of Carlow's full-time faculty, a majority of support staff leadership, and a substantial number of student leaders. At the end of the day, the attendees reached consensus agreement on a set of institutional learning outcomes that reflected the unique nature of the Carlow learning experience. Examples include ethical and social responsibility and creative thinking. The University Faculty Assembly formally approved the learning outcomes at the beginning of the next semester.

Principle 3: Collaborative

The momentum and energy of this inclusive effort translated to assessment of these outcomes in the spring 2014 semester, identification of gaps where the outcomes were not adequately supported within the existing curriculum, and a complete redesign of the general education experience based on the results of these assessments. The new general education curriculum, dubbed the Carlow Compass, was approved by the University Faculty Assembly in spring 2015 and officially launched in fall 2016.

The Carlow Learning Outcomes (CLOs) now serve as the bedrock of the Compass Curriculum. Every course approved within the Compass Curriculum must identify within its syllabus how it embeds and assesses relevant CLOs. Specifically, (a) Which CLO(s) will the students develop? (b) How will the students learn them? and (c) How will they demonstrate them? At the end of each semester, Compass Curriculum instructors submit their course-level assessment results for each of the embedded CLOs to a Compass Steering Committee composed of faculty members from each of Carlow's three colleges, the Compass director, and the director of assessment. The Compass Steering Committee then identifies trends within the results and uses this information to produce recommendations to improve student learning and develop new methods of support for a cohort of students as that cohort progresses to the next tier of the Compass Curriculum.

Principle 5: Responsive to students' needs in the present tense

Principle 4: Anchored in continuous reporting and acting on assessment results

Ultimately, the Carlow Compass Curriculum culminates in a specially designed Junior Anchor Course, which is a common touchpoint for all students in the first semester of their junior year. Through this course, every student completes a high-level project that incorporates CLOs in an integrative way. Through this project, students' proficiencies with each

CLO are assessed. If any deficiencies are noted (e.g., with written communication skills), students are referred to campus support services for additional attention and support. This experience is designed to capture all student populations—undergraduate students who pass through all years of the curriculum as well as transfer students who arrive at Carlow with a significant amount of general education credits.

Assessing Student Learning Within Disciplinary Programs

To implement its new assessment framework within individual programs of study, Carlow University relied on a system of transparent milestones and open accountability. At the beginning, Carlow's assessment committee—made up of respected faculty and staff representatives—worked with the Office of Institutional Research, Effectiveness, and Planning to clearly describe assessment expectations for each program and translate them into practical implementation milestones. The resulting 11 common milestones encompassed everything from receiving a formal introduction to the assessment expectations, developing an assessment plan, and receiving training on an information management system (TracDat) to be able to enter plans, results, and corresponding actions into that system. In the first year of implementing program-level assessment in the disciplines, a group of pilot programs openly tracked their progress and shared that progress through a chart displayed at every University Faculty Assembly meeting. Visually, the chart listed each program along with corresponding milestone progress bars. Each program's progress bar was **Principle 4: Anchored in continuous reporting of and acting on assessment results** shaded Carlow purple wherever a corresponding milestone was completed. The pilot programs, consisting of 19 of Carlow's 46 degree-granting programs, served as exemplars for all other programs. At each update, faculty could see their peers' achievements and challenges. It encouraged candid and constructive conversations. The process resulted in a combination of performance anxiety, pride, and progress. Faculty increasingly made a game of "getting their purple," representing attainment of a program-level milestone. In the first year, programs representing more than half of the student population fully closed the assessment loop. In two years, 18 of the 19 pilot programs fully closed the loop. After the pilot year, all remaining programs joined and have since achieved progress at the same rate and to the same extent.

At the beginning and end of each semester, the director of assessment meets with the provost and each college dean to review an assessment dashboard and discuss areas that merit attention. The dashboard summarizes each program's performance in the following areas: (a) the quality of its current assessment plans (based on an assessment plan evaluation rubric) and (b) the extent to which each program has successfully documented closing the loop within the TracDat system (entered results, actions, and follow-ups about action implementation). The provost, deans, and director of assessment review the dashboard highlights and collaboratively determine ways to support programs and bring them to higher levels of proficiency in their engagement with the learning assessment process. At a more granular level, the assessment plan evaluation rubric is used to provide feedback and recommendations to individual programs about steps they can take to improve their learning assessment processes. Following this, the director of assessment and/or respective dean meet directly with program staff to ensure they have plans in place for addressing any areas where assessment results indicate that attention is necessary.

Principle 4: Anchored in continuous reporting and acting on assessment results

Principle 3: Collaborative

Principle 5: Responsive to students' needs in the present tense

In terms of institutional support and value of assessment, the academic leadership has recognized that true impact comes from true resource commitment—time being one of the most important resources. In acknowledgment, the administration has carved out calendar space: a Close the Loop Day at the end and an Open the Loop Day at the beginning of each academic year. During these days, faculty are given uninhibited time to organize and analyze assessment results, engage with their colleagues in discussions about learning, and ensure actions are in place to address areas in need of improvement before the next semester begins. Breakfast, lunch, open meeting spaces, and technology support are provided. Most importantly, on-demand consulting is available from each of the college deans and the Office of Institutional Research, Effectiveness, and Planning.

Principle 6: Institutionally valued through resources, support, and recognition of time needed to develop and implement timely interventions

These are the threads Carlow has used to weave a strong culture of assessment. Grounded in mission and focused on learning, assessment has served as a catalyst for change and actualization of institutional values.

Note. Contributed by August C. Delbert, director of assessment, institutional research, effectiveness, and planning; and Anne M. Candreva, assistant vice president, institutional research, effectiveness, and planning, Carlow University. Used with permission.

Case 4.3. The University of St. Augustine for Health Sciences: Assessment as a Call to Action at the University

Case 4.3 shows how the University of St. Augustine for Health Sciences (USAHS), a graduate institution, has engaged internal stakeholders at multiple levels to develop and sustain real-time student assessment. A mission that includes acknowledging the importance of individualized education to enable its diverse students to achieve high-quality professional licensure or certification drives this commitment. Inclusive and collaborative processes have emerged to develop a shared continuous commitment to identify and address patterns of students' underperformance. One process involved developing and calibrating agreed-upon scoring rubrics—designed internally as well as adapted from the VALUE rubrics. Another process involved developing interrater reliability to achieve consistency in scoring student work. Patterns of underperformance are tracked across various learning contexts in face-to-face or online learning modes. Several examples, such as how a pattern of underperformance in students' writing was addressed, illustrate timely interventions. The institution's semester commitment to assessment planning and formal program review processes engages faculty, staff, and administrators, representing an inclusive commitment to enrolled students' success. There are two other keys to this institution's ability to sustain real-time student assessment. First, the Office of Assessment and Institutional Research and the Department of Educational Effectiveness support gathering evidence of student learning and using results continually to educate constituencies about efficacious educational practices or the need to develop innovative ones. Second, the institution's current and evolving reward system values those who advance this learner-centered institutional commitment.

CASE 4.3.

The University of St. Augustine for Health Sciences Assessment as a Call to Action at the University

The University of St. Augustine for Health Sciences (USAHS) is a graduate institution with a mission to develop "professional health care practitioners through innovative, individualized and quality classroom, clinical and distance educations" (usa.edu/p11-249-About-the-University.aspx).

USAHS's two largest programs are its doctor of physical therapy program and its master of occupational therapy program. Maintaining a low student-to-faculty ratio throughout its 40-year history, enrollment across three campuses at USAHS is currently just under 2,000 students for eight degree programs. There are aspirations to grow and add new programs, and the university plans to open a fourth campus in the very near future.

Unique to its mission and aligned with its core value of promoting excellence in education, assessment efforts at USAHS are driven internally by a strong desire to ensure that its students exhibit professionalism and integrity and adhere to ethical standards. High pass rates on licensure and certification examinations across campuses are of paramount importance, so these parameters are continuously monitored to identify and rectify any disparities in achievement of learning that may arise by campus, respective of enrollment, mode of course delivery, age, gender, or race/ethnicity.

Principle 1: Internally driven by the institution's focus on preparing professionals across diverse populations and modes of delivery

In order to ensure a shared commitment to equitable and measurable progress toward achievement of learning outcomes for high-quality degrees, the university engages its faculty, staff, and administrators in formal assessment planning and program review processes each term. The Office of Assessment and Institutional Research was formed in 2013 with a mission to provide support in gathering evidence, implementing best practices, and enhancing overall educational effectiveness. The Department of Educational Effectiveness was formed in 2014 to lead efforts and offer faculty development opportunities to advance excellence in learning and promote innovative teaching strategies with all faculty.

Assessing Student Learning

Through a highly focused and cooperative process across campuses and in online sections, the faculty of the critical thinking/clinical reasoning courses in conjunction with the faculty of research-based courses quickly identified, through assessment, that students tended to struggle with the Sources and Evidence component of our written communication competency rubric adapted from AAC&U's corresponding VALUE

Principle 5: Responsive to students' needs in the present tense

rubric. This identification led to an orchestrated effort by the Office of Assessment and Institutional Research and select faculty to facilitate structured workshops with facilitated dialogue to heighten the likelihood for both increased intra-rater consistency and interrater reliability. To be responsive to students' needs, one faculty member pioneered a pilot teaching-learning strategy to advance written communication competency for select student cohorts in the doctor of physical therapy program. Students were actively encouraged to participate in five structured writing lessons as well as three two-hour writing workshops in one term. Preliminary results revealed that those students who were exposed to the pilot teaching-learning strategy scored higher on their end-of-term written communication competency for several criteria compared with levels at which they were assessed when the term began.

Involvement at Multiple Levels

Inclusivity, when it comes to outcome assessment, was forefront for the assessment team, and it became more than what was initially planned for the university. First, the VALUE rubrics were shared and continue to be shared with all students prior to their use with any assignment in any course. Contributing faculty may now also join core faculty in assessing any particular competency respective of an identified assignment in any course. Thus, assessment is no longer limited to only a small group of faculty; it occurs at multiple levels, and involvement is also at multiple levels within the university.

Principle 2: Inclusive of faculty, staff, and assessment professionals

As part of an inclusive assessment process at multiple levels, the cocurricular effectiveness subcommittee piloted an ePortfolio containing a self-reflective writing component for its graduating physical therapy students on the St. Augustine campus. The committee—comprising assessment professionals, faculty in physical and occupational therapy, and staff—collaboratively developed an analytic rubric and a set of instructional materials for students. Reflecting on their participation in wellness activities, community service, student associations, and advocacy, students submitted artifacts that revealed evidence of deep connected learning. The project led to authentic assessment of collaborative leadership abilities, communication, and a formative sense of professionalism.

Adopting a criterion-referenced approach to rubric-based assessment represented an advancement for the university. The outcomes assessment coordinator worked closely with faculty, program directors, and deans in an interdepartmental effort to contextualize, implement, and calibrate analytic rubrics for use in coursework in numerous courses within any one program. Through a highly collaborative process, the written communication competency skills of students on a signature assignment in a common critical thinking course were piloted and assessed longitudinally by core and contributing faculty over a period of multiple trimesters. Initially, when the rubrics were piloted, high variability in scoring was revealed and norming workshops were created. As a result of the norming workshops, genuine dialogue emerged about the expectations for scholarly writing, an inherently

Principle 3: Collaborative

complex endeavor for any graduate student. In a similar project, an inter-departmental team of faculty from doctors of physical therapy, orthopedic assistants, and librarians across all campuses collaborated to assess students' information literacy skills. A series of facilitated norming workshops was conducted virtually following processes described by Maki (2004), leading to (a) formal determinations of interrater reliability, (b) productive conversations around standards of judgment of student performance in research-based coursework, and (c) efforts to build a scholarship of assessment at the university.

The university leverages the use of LiveText—an assessment management system—as a tool for assessing student work and generating reports for single and multiple raters. Assessment data are collected and stored in real time in a highly transparent and robust manner. Each student is provided with the results of his or her key assessments. Reports are generated at the course, program, and institutional level and aligned to the university's expectations for graduate learning. When norming the written communication rubric, faculty expressed that the immediacy of formative feedback was helpful to students so that the students could ultimately prepare work in the immediate future to meet target levels of performance.

Principle 5: Responsive to students' needs in the present tense

Principle 4: Anchored in continuous reporting and acting on assessment results

To assess proficiency longitudinally, a rubric was shared with the students in their first trimester and used to assess their performance on a different assignment four trimesters later. An optional writing workshop was offered that enabled an analysis of comparative performance for those who had opted to attend the workshop against those who did not.

Additionally, in the Critical Thinking I course, students were provided with the rubric, and their performance was assessed at two points in a single trimester. In this way, the faculty were able to determine the effectiveness of a writing intervention and communicate expectations. Students gained a heightened understanding and awareness of their writing skill set and certainly elevated their written communication competency on the next assignment.

Shaping and Directing the Future

After nearly two years of piloting, contextualizing, and calibrating AAC&U's information literacy and written communication VALUE rubrics (Rhodes, 2010) for graduate-level work, the performance of approximately 900 students at three campuses across two programs has been completed and has been included in the institution's annual reports. To further encourage faculty participation and successful implementation, USAHS also started an award system, and in early 2015, the university awarded its first Faculty Assessment 1.0 Award. This award provides special recognition for an individual who effectively uses results to drive improvements in learning and teaching. Another criterion is engagement, meaning that this faculty member motivates other faculty members and helps fellow faculty with their assessment efforts. In addition, the award winner was recognized for the ability to communicate the purpose and use of the assessment rubric to students. The first awards went to faculty members who pioneered the use of rubrics in their critical thinking class with particular assignments. This award was also symbolic, to say the least, and in essence recognized that assessment, using rubrics, would become a part of the university's teaching culture going forward.

Principle 6: Institutionally valued through an award system

The implementation of an award system at the institution level clearly demonstrates to its learning community how much assessment is valued at the institution. This award program is the first of many to follow. In fact, the Assessment 1.0 Program has set the stage for the university's next innovative award program, a recognized badging system. This badging system will initially recognize individuals with outstanding achievement not only in assessment but also in two new competency areas: (a) teaching and learning and (b) peer mentoring.

Note. Contributed by David J. Turbow, assessment coordinator, Office of Assessment and Institutional Research; and Thomas P. Werner, assistant director, Flex DPT Program, University of St. Augustine for Health Sciences. Used with permission.

Case 4.4. Salem State University's Occupational Therapy Program: Current Academic Year Assessment Timetable

Case 4.4 illustrates the current academic year assessment timetable that faculty in Salem State University's Occupational Therapy (OT) program annually and collaboratively follow. It enables administrators and faculty to gauge continuously students' progress toward achieving high-quality program-level outcomes. Moreover, it identifies the need to develop real-time interventions to improve currently enrolled students' patterns of underperformance as soon as they occur or as they persist. The academic year assessment timetable begins with baseline data from a competency-based test that all entering students take to identify their strengths and weaknesses. Faculty collectively learn about those patterns before students take their first courses. This knowledge is especially important given the diversity of the university's student body, including low-income and first-generation students. Students themselves simultaneously learn about their entering patterns of performance and underperformance—a baseline that holds students accountable for their academic progress. Faculty closely follow each student's progress at specific times in a semester. Developments of real-time interventions or practices in a semester as well as across all semesters help students improve patterns of weakness to keep them on track to degree completion. End-of-year assessment data include yet another opportunity to identify remaining weak patterns in student work. Faculty also score students' annual ePortfolio entries, demonstrating students' progress toward or achievement of program-level outcomes.

CASE 4.4.
Continuous Assessment of Student Learning in Salem State University's Occupational Therapy Program

1. **Prior to taking courses in the major**, students are tested on a set of required competencies. Students and faculty are given feedback on students' areas of strengths and weaknesses.
2. **During each semester**, faculty meetings are held weekly to discuss any curricular or student issues in courses. Modifications are made as indicated from faculty feedback.
3. **At midsemester**, professional behavior assessments (PBA) are completed by faculty on every student in each class and shared with the student. If a student is doing poorly on the PBA the faculty and student develop goals to improve by the end of the semester when the PBA is completed again by the faculty member.
4. **At the end of the semester**, students and faculty complete specific departmental course assessments. These data are compiled by the faculty assessment committee and presented at the end-of-the-semester faculty retreat. These data are used to make necessary modifications to the curriculum design, content, scope, and sequencing of courses to ensure a quality education program for its students. Professional behavior assessments are also completed at the end of the semester and shared with students. Those students who do not pass the PBA meet with the chairperson, fieldwork coordinator, faculty member

who gave the assessment, and the graduate coordinator if he or she is in the master's program to develop a behavior action plan that the student must follow to progress in the program.

5. **End-of-year** data are gathered from the capstone assignments and the ePortfolios students complete. Students build their ePortfolios over the entire time they are in the program. They self-select authentic pieces of evidence of their learning that they believe meet the program's learning outcomes and upload them into their ePortfolio on Canvas. Faculty and students give and receive feedback on their ePortfolios during their capstone course. Faculty then score the student portfolios with outcome rubrics loaded on Canvas. These data are then compiled, and student learning is assessed against the benchmarks set in the OT evaluation plan. This information is shared with faculty at the end-of-the-year summits.

6. **At external assessment of student learning times**, each student in the program develops, implements, and presents a research project at a student-run research conference.

Note. Contributed by Jeramie Silveira, graduate coordinator in occupational therapy and faculty assessment fellow at Salem State University. Shared in communication with author in February 2015. Used with permission.

The Relevance of Real-Time Student Assessment

Real-time student assessment is internally driven by the need to know how well all students are progressing toward achieving a high-quality degree. Compared with scheduled wait-and-see or delayed-response assessment approaches that occur between longer periods of time, real-time assessment closes those gaps to target currently enrolled students' equitable progress toward long-term success. Extending time to learn about students' levels of performance reduces an institution's and its programs' capacity to

- close gaps in achievement for all currently enrolled students;
- keep currently enrolled students on track to degree completion;
- measurably improve graduation rates for historically underrepresented students; and
- measurably improve well-documented, persistent undergraduate patterns of underperformance in general education outcomes such as critical thinking, writing, and analysis.

Posting end-of-semester course- or educational experience–based assessment results provides an institution and its programs with formative evidence of how well currently enrolled students are progressing toward attaining a high-quality degree. Cycles of assessment or other point-in-time approaches using scoring rubrics to report students' progress focus only on those students who have made it to those points in time—the survivors. Without a trace, the specific academic challenges of individual students who dropped out, withdrew, or failed disappear in reported assessment results. Comparing real-time assessment with more commonly used delayed-response assessment approaches, as illustrated in Table 4.1, heightens the relevance of real-time assessment for institutions that are serious about closing achievement gaps, measurably improving graduation rates across historically underrepresented students, and preparing all currently enrolled students with the outcomes they need to be active and productive citizens.

Real-time assessment drives the need for agility—developing on-time interventions or new practices that enable currently enrolled students to overcome the range of barriers or challenges they face as they learn. Evidence of the efficacy of on-time interventions or new practices is documented in semester-by-semester dashboard reporting (sometimes in midsemester reporting). In contrast to assessment cycles and point-in-time assessment approaches, real-time student assessment serves as the catalyst for taking actions in the present tense as opposed to sometime in the future. And that future may be extended based on time for deliberations, decision-making, and even the actual implementation of an agreed-upon intervention or new practices that likely do not immediately benefit currently enrolled students. In contrast, the sets of interventions or practices that are developed in real time to improve currently enrolled students' performance can also be used to advance future students.

Chapter 5 focuses on how developments in technology are contributing to real-time student assessment, improving on-time access to and analysis of assessment results.

TABLE 4.1

Real-Time Assessment Compared With Cycles of Assessment or Point-in-Time Assessment Approaches

Real-Time Student Assessment	Cycles of Assessment or Point-in-Time Assessment Approaches
Who Benefits?	**Who Benefits?**
Currently enrolled students are the direct beneficiaries. Real-time student assessment documents each student's progress, identifying • individuals or cohorts who are struggling, and • patterns of underperformance that need to be addressed on time and over time. Real-time student assessment closes time gaps between assessment cycles or other scheduled point-in-time assessment approaches, enabling stakeholders to learn continuously about all students' progress toward attaining a degree. Thus, it represents a longitudinal commitment to students' equitable success by engaging faculty and other internal stakeholders in attending to the specific obstacles or challenges students face as they learn.	Future students are typically the beneficiaries. Assessment cycles or other point-in-time assessment approaches represent wait-and-see approaches that occur at designated times and often to satisfy external mandates. These approaches take snapshots of students who persist—the survivors—ignoring the students who dropped out or failed and the specific academic challenges they faced. They represent an uneven commitment to students' equitable success by disengaging faculty and other internal stakeholders from addressing the obstacles or challenges students face as they progress course-by-course to attain a degree. The extreme example of point-in-time assessment occurs in programs that assess students' achievement at one time only: near graduation. These approaches extend the time to learn about students' patterns of underperformance that could have been identified and addressed when they first occurred or as they persisted. Further, point-in-time assessment and cycles of assessment are not focused on students' equitable improvement but rather on generalizing about persisting students' overall performance.

(Continues)

TABLE 4.1 (*Continued*)

Real-Time Student Assessment	Cycles of Assessment or Point-in-Time Assessment Approaches
Who Interrogates Assessment Results?	**Who Interrogates Assessment Results?**
Real-time assessment involves full participation of faculty at the program level and participation of faculty contributing to general education at the institution level. Interrogation of disaggregated assessment results at one or more times in an academic year (sometimes even at points in a semester) occurs within the context of specific courses and educational experiences. Faculty and other contributors to student learning, including individuals from an institution's network of experts, interrogate assessment results to identify continuously short- and long-term interventions or practices to improve student learning. Interrogating assessment results with colleagues and relevant members of an institution's network of experts broadens discussion of the sets of strategies or practices to address entrenched or persistent patterns of underperformance. Many of these patterns cannot be improved in "one more course"; they can be improved over time with chronological practice in a range of contexts and consistent feedback to students. Collaboration across the curriculum and cocurriculum is essential to improve persistent patterns of underperformance, such as in critical thinking or writing.	Point-in-time assessment involves limited or uneven participation of faculty based on the purpose of assessment: to report findings at a point in time to satisfy external demands or report on students' learning gains at a specific point in time. Interrogating assessment results may occur well beyond the time that student work is collected and scored in contrast to real-time assessment, which reports and acts on results at specific times in an academic year. Interrogation is based primarily on the course or courses from which student work is collected at a designated time, absent previous relevant chronological results that may have identified those underperformance patterns earlier. Methods of collecting student work for point-in-time assessment vary, such as collecting all student work from a designated course or courses, collecting some student work from a designated course or courses depending on who will volunteer that work, and sampling of student work—especially prevalent at high-enrollment institutions. Those whose work is sampled represent those who persist. Further, those whose work is sampled may not accurately represent an institution's student demographics, severely limiting an institution's capacity to close measurably time to degree and gaps in achievement and graduation rates. Time gaps between assessment periods represent lost opportunities to address and continually improve patterns of underperformance.

When Are Actions Implemented to Improve Student Learning?	When Are Actions Implemented to Improve Student Learning?
Results are reported and acted on each semester or between other short intervals of time to address currently enrolled students' patterns of underperformance when they occur and as they persist. Proposed actions to improve learning are discussed among colleagues within the following contexts: (a) specific context of a course, module, or education experience and (b) subsequent courses, modules, or education experiences that build on students' previous learning. Thus, there is a longitudinal context within which underperformance patterns need to be addressed: expectations for students as they progress toward program- and degree-level expectations. For example, students' lack of conceptual understanding at the end of their first- or second-year physics major limits their successful achievement in higher-level courses unless patterns of misunderstanding are addressed early on or continue to be addressed in subsequent courses.	Results are reported and acted on at the end of a point in time or a cycle of assessment. Some cycles address one or a set of outcomes; each cycle can take as long as one or more years to complete. For example, if an institution has eight general education outcomes, then it may take eight years to assess all outcomes one-by-one. Extended assessment cycles separate discussions about actions to improve learning from students' specific contexts for learning, resulting in more general interventions or recommendations to improve student learning.
	Interventions or new practices identified after prolonged assessment cycles, after long gaps between cycles, or limited to assessing students' near-graduation work benefit future students rather than currently enrolled students. An assumption underlying wait-and-see assessment approaches is that future students will have the same set of underperformance patterns as those who were assessed the year or years before. Students are not standardized.
Real-time reporting of assessment requires resiliency; results drive nimble actions to improve students' progress continuously along their educational pathways. Improving student learning occurs over time—a shared, not a siloed, commitment to students' success.	Delayed reporting of assessment results leads to delayed implemented actions to improve currently enrolled students' learning. Delayed reporting may also trigger some institutions and programs to develop near-graduation catch-up intervention strategies that benefit those who make it to the end. If student work is assessed from a near-graduation course, such as a capstone, proposed interventions to improve underperformance patterns might focus only on how to improve student learning in that particular course. Patterns of underperformance should be identified and addressed early in students' studies as well as along the trajectory of their studies to determine their abilities to achieve expected high-quality program and degree outcomes in their capstone course.

(Continues)

TABLE 4.1 *(Continued)*

Real-Time Student Assessment	Cycles of Assessment or Point-in-Time Assessment Approaches
How Do Internal Stakeholders Remain Continuously Informed About and Responsive to Students' Equitable Progress Toward Attaining a High-Quality Degree?	**How Do Internal Stakeholders Remain Continuously Informed About and Responsive to Students' Equitable Progress Toward Attaining a High-Quality Degree?**
Continuous semester postings of demographically disaggregated course and education experience assessment results provide a shared gauge for internal stakeholders to remain informed about and continuously responsive to currently enrolled students' academic needs. That footing is necessary to close achievement and graduation gaps continuously and measurably across an institution's student demographics.	Delayed postings of assessment results provide documentation of retained students' progress or near-graduation achievement levels, often based on sampling. Thus, these data do not reflect a shared commitment to students' equitable progress. Focus remains only on those students who persist. Delayed postings may or may not be readily or consistently available to all faculty and other contributors to student learning. Interrogating data reported in delayed postings leads to more general interventions for future students than the context-specific continuous interventions identified in real-time assessment.

TECHNOLOGY THAT CONTRIBUTES TO REAL-TIME STUDENT ASSESSMENT

Current and emerging developments and refinements in technology are expanding opportunities for students to learn, demonstrate their learning, and receive timely assessment of their performance, sometimes even displayed on their mobile devices. At the same time, developments and refinements in technology are expanding opportunities for internal stakeholders to access, analyze, and act in real time on evidence of student learning and other institutional data that identify additional factors that affect students' progress and persistence. Among all these developments, some of which are still emerging on the higher education landscape, this chapter provides a brief overview of the following five types of technology that contribute to an institution's commitment to real-time assessment:

1. learning management systems (LMSs) or other platforms that collect, synthesize, sort, and report real-time assessment results;
2. assessment management systems (AMSs) that also perform those tasks for an entire institution and its programs;
3. adaptive learning platforms that individualize instruction by addressing learner challenges and report on students' progress and final performance;
4. web-based education data-mining tools that provide new insights into institutional-, program-, and student-level variables that affect students' progress or are predictive of their continued success; and
5. ePortfolios that provide a shared means for faculty, other contributors to student learning, and students themselves to gauge continuously

students' equitable progress toward attaining high-quality institution- and program-level outcomes.

Although these technological options are discussed separately to provide readers with a sense of their individual capacities, they are not necessarily stand-alone options, as several case studies will illustrate. For example, most AMSs also offer an ePortfolio platform and may use the analytics capacity of technology to report assessment results. Though still emerging on the landscape of higher education, some LMSs draw on adaptive learning technology in the instructional design of courses and modules and on learning analytics technology to monitor and report students' performance levels. LMSs may also offer ePortfolio platforms. Altogether these technological options facilitate access to and analysis of real-time data. Some resources to guide further campus inquiry into these types of educational technology are listed at the end of this chapter.

Learning Management Systems or Other Platforms

LMSs or other platforms that collect and disseminate assessment results have a range of features that contribute to real-time assessment, including synthesizing, aggregating and disaggregating, and displaying assessment results in visual formats. Case 5.1 describes how the real-time reporting capacity of an LMS supports the institution's tracking of students' progress toward achieving five of its six general education outcomes. Case 5.2 illustrates the way faculty and other contributors to student learning in a major program collaboratively use a software system that collects and disseminates different kinds of student data to gauge students' real-time progress toward achieving program-level outcomes and take action to improve patterns of underperformance as they emerge in students' work. Both cases also document how students learn about their progress.

Using the Desire2Learn (D2L) LMS, multiple stakeholders at the University of Central Oklahoma (UCO) are now monitoring undergraduate students' progress toward achieving five of the university's six core learning outcomes through its Student Transformative Learning Record (STLR). Badge levels are determined based on agreed-upon criteria. As Case 5.1 describes, faculty and other contributors to student learning, such as student affairs and residence life professionals, have designed STLR assignments that extend students' learning of those outcomes beyond courses in the core curriculum. They provide students with multiple other opportunities to achieve the institution's highest level of performance. Students' progress is a shared commitment, not a siloed commitment.

CASE 5.1.
Student Transformative Learning Record (STLR): Assessment and Documentation of Student Learning Related to High-Impact Practices at the University of Central Oklahoma

Since 2007 at the University of Central Oklahoma, we have proclaimed six central tenets of transformative learning as our approach to high-impact practices. The tenets are discipline knowledge; leadership; research, creative, and scholarly activity; global and cultural competencies; service-learning and civic engagement; and health and wellness. For several years, there were many conversations about how to assess and document this learning; many faculty and professional staff could describe in detail the learning they had observed in individual students. We knew it was happening, but we did not have an effective strategy for assessment.

In fall 2012, a group of us began weekly project meetings with the goal of creating one system through which we could assess and document student learning and, in the process, engage students in articulating their achievements. The work group consisted of representatives from academic affairs, institutional effectiveness, the center for teaching and learning, information technology, and student affairs. The key to the success of these early conversations was collaboration among these units. Several months into the project, the emphasis was clearly and consistently on what and how students were learning and seldom on where or by whom they were taught.

The scheme, as it emerged, would be implemented through our learning management system, D2L/Brightspace (D2L), and would include learning that happened in classes as well as through activities in student life, residence life, and other out-of-classroom venues. Assignments within classes are designated as Student Transformative Learning Record (STLR) assignments, and instructors grade student work on a rubric specific to that assignment and then evaluate the student's achievement of one or more of the central six tenets (five, actually, as there are no badges for discipline knowledge at this point; it is assumed that the academic transcript expresses competence in a student's major) on a rubric at one of three badge levels: exposure, integration, and transformation. In the case of student activities, course shells are created within the LMS for each activity, and assessment of student performance and badge levels are selected the same way as for class assignments.

D2L holds all student artifacts and assessments and provides the documentation of student progress. Each time a student's work is assessed, the student can choose to push that piece of work, with the assessment, to the ePortfolio. (Only at the exposure level do students get STLR designations without an assessment; they might attend a presentation related to global competence, where, just by sliding their ID card, attendance is recorded through D2L as exposure.) Within the ePortfolio, the student can organize the STLR activities to best represent learning and accomplishments, creating "presentations" for job or graduate school applications, for instance. In D2L, the ePortfolio is accessible to the student and only the student; we cannot get assessment information from the ePortfolios. Instead, we work through the competency structure in D2L; for each tenet, the connections are made between each badge level and the scoring rubric. The STLR project team can extract reports from D2L that tell us how many students have participated in STLR activities and assignments, in each of the five tenets, and the badge level that each was awarded. In this way, we can gauge the degree to which students are engaged in each of our transformative learning tenets and to what depth. We are hoping to see a pattern that shows mostly exposure badges in the first year, increasing in the second year to include integration, and then, in the junior and senior years, to see a greater number of transformation badges in the mix.

During the first semester that we piloted the scheme with about 200 students and about 20 instructors and professional staff in student affairs, we received a $7.8 million Title III grant for STLR implementation. The grant is for five years, and about a third of the money goes directly to students in stipends for undergraduate research efforts, internship opportunities, and independent projects in collaboration with faculty or professional staff. There is money for faculty and professional staff training stipends; for grant personnel travel and resources; for participation in conferences; and for personnel to manage the assessment and documentation of student learning, the technological requirements in the LMS, and the major challenge of training faculty, professional staff, and students.

We have started with instructors in the first-year experience program and in general education courses that are taken by most first-year students. In classes, there are STLR-designated assignments, so students will begin to accumulate points toward their badges by attending classes and completing assignments. These might include a required service-learning project, a behavior change project in our required health and wellness class, or a speech in an oral communication class on a topic with a global or cultural theme. In addition, many student activities are open for student participation, from attending an event highlighting a specific culture to serving in student government to heading up a student organization.

In their first years, students will be engaged in a variety of assignments and experiences, mostly, we anticipate, at the exposure level. Through these early experiences, a student might become more deeply engaged in one or two areas and begin to specialize and move into deeper learning that would reach the integration level. In a proposal that came out of the AAC&U Institute on General Education Assessment, one of our emphases will be to encourage instructors of core general education courses to include an STLR assignment in each class. In addition, we want to distribute general education more evenly across a student's four years, so that students encounter gradually more complex and engaging assignments.

The rubric for leadership (Table 5.1.1), describes how a student might progress from lacking belief in ability to serve as a leader to assuming a community leadership position that involves drawing on the talents of others.

TABLE 5.1.1
STLR Badge Level Descriptors for Leadership

	Transformation	*Integration*	*Exposure*	*NOT*
Leadership	The student can identify the leadership styles and philosophies of peers and effectively use this knowledge to create teams and workgroups. The student is cognizant of community needs and aligns her or his efforts to serve and meet those needs.	The student articulates a personal philosophy of leadership. The student acknowledges that individuals may display leadership differently and recognizes that leadership is not a position or title but centers on the ability to influence the community (world).	The student may have never considered her- or himself as a leader but is open to the potential and understands that each person has the ability to serve as a leader. The student may have begun to develop an awareness of her or his own personal values and how they differ from those of others. The student interacts with others who are considered leaders and may adopt the mind-set of serving as a leader with a position or title in limited experiences or activities.	The student believes that she or he does not have the potential to serve as a leader and seems unwilling to explore the opportunities presented.

Note. Contributed by Cia Verschelden, executive director, institutional assessment, University of Central Oklahoma. Used with permission.

At Bridgewater State University, the Counselor Education Program has adapted a software program, Qualtrics, to accommodate the needs of faculty, students, and on-site supervisors as students progress through their program, semester-by-semester. The system enables dissemination of assessment results that are used comprehensively to improve student learning in real time.

CASE 5.2.
Bridgewater State University: Customizing an Existing Platform to Facilitate Real-Time Program-Level Assessment

The Qualtrics Platform

Bridgewater State University, the largest university in the Massachusetts State University System, enrolls a combined total of 11,187 graduate and undergraduate students as of fall 2015 and uses Qualtrics, an institutionally funded online survey software system, for most of its indirect assessment needs. However, the robustness of the tool also allows for customized projects for direct assessment similar to Tk20, Taskstream, and Digication. Qualtrics offers a low-tech design platform that is faculty-friendly and data rich. One example of how a department is using program-level assessment to drive real-time student success is in the counselor education program.

Real-Time Reporting

Initially, the first set of web-based surveys developed by the faculty to track students' course-by-course progress in reaching exit-level outcomes is used to provide immediate feedback to students on their progress toward program completion and also to serve as a data-driven mechanism for continuous program improvement.

A second set of surveys is used for every semester that students are active interns in the field. Information is gathered from these students and their site supervisors through electronically distributed midterm and final evaluations. These evaluations are managed and downloaded by a staff member and distributed to faculty and students as individual reports. Discussions among the instructor, site supervisor, and student occur throughout the semester to explore and identify competencies toward which students are demonstrating progress and existing learning gaps.

A third survey focused on program evaluation occurs at the end of the semester. Program evaluations are electronically sent to site supervisors who provide feedback on how well the program prepares students for their internship role. These data are shared with faculty for review. Based on areas identified as needing improvement—such as course content, pedagogy, dissemination of course materials, and fieldwork structures or processes—adjustments are made to increase student success.

Finally, a fourth survey, administered to all students in the counselor education program in the fall and spring semesters, is used to gain input about program design, faculty instruction, academic advising, course workload, and students' overall experience in the program.

All four assessments provide valuable data on students' mastery of the competencies required for a graduate degree in counselor education and align with the requirements specified by the Council for Accreditation of Counseling and Related Educational Programs (CACREP). While not as sophisticated as other technology-enabled assessment systems like Desire2Learn, Qualtrics is a relatively low-cost, high-value assessment tool. Students gain timely feedback on their academic performance and the department gains a set of data analytics to make informed decisions about continuous program improvement focused on improving student success. Similar on-time assessment projects are being piloted in social work and early childhood education, both heavily reliant on helping students integrate course content with applied field-based experiences.

Note. Contributed by Amanda Barudin, director of fieldwork and staff associate for counselor education; and Ruth Slotnick, director of assessment, Bridgewater State University.

AMSs

Initially, AMSs were designed to support and document institutional efforts to assess students' learning. For that purpose, these systems include protocols or formats, such as curriculum maps, to help internal stakeholders demonstrate to accreditors their institution- and program-level commitments to assessment. What became especially noteworthy over time was that most of these systems developed and integrated ePortfolio platforms, providing a place for students to upload their work. Responding to the rising demand to assess and improve students' learning of general education and program-level outcomes, AMSs—such as Tk20, AcademicEffect (previously WEAVEonline), Taskstream, LiveText, eLumen, TracDat, Digication, Chalk & Wire, and Nuventive—downloaded accreditors' standards to help faculty and administrators align courses and assignments with those standards. Since 2005 these systems have also downloaded LEAP outcomes and DQP proficiencies, as well as downloaded VALUE rubrics so that there is a shared means to score student work documenting achievement of one or more general education outcomes.

Contributing to internal stakeholders' real-time access to and collaborative analysis of assessment results are web-based performance dashboards integrated into AMSs. These dashboards report real-time results of scoring students' authentic work or results based on other metrics built into an AMS. Recent developments in these dashboards now provide internal stakeholders with optional visual representations of assessment results that assist real-time interrogation of results, including along demographic lines. Assessment results can be aggregated and disaggregated in multiple ways, such as at the level of individual student performance in a course, at the level of all students' comparative performance in a course, and at the level of all students' performance in courses having the same outcome and using the same metric. Figure 5.1, a screenshot of a drill-down interactive dashboard option, illustrates one way that Tk20 displays Critical Thinking VALUE rubric scores for students' work in a single course.

In this screenshot, quantitative results at the top of the screen report students' overall achievement against the Critical Thinking VALUE rubric criteria. Accompanying these results is a visual representation of students' progress toward achieving the highest level of each criterion, represented in the lower part of the screenshot. This filter, among many others in the Tk20 system, also enables stakeholders to view all sections of a course, such as all foundational composition sections that assess critical thinking, and continues to track how well students progress in their achievement of critical thinking and other outcomes along the trajectory of their learning. That longitudinal commitment becomes the means for the institution and its programs to identify and then address continuously persistent patterns of underperformance. Most important, taking a longitudinal view of students' achievement levels sustains a shared focus on students' equitable progress toward achieving high-quality program and degree outcomes.

Figures 5.2, 5.3, and 5.4 illustrate and describe some of the possible visual displays available in Taskstream's Aqua AMS that provide options for viewing students' performance of an outcome in multiple courses. In these figures, dashboard assessment results are displayed based on assignments in five specific first-year courses that require students to demonstrate the criteria in the VALUE written communication rubric. It is important to note that users can also import other options to filter assessment results, such as student demographics, to track specific student cohorts' progress. Figure 5.2 illustrates the option "all criteria" of viewing students' average performance in writing under each criterion. Figure 5.3 provides another option, "score distribution by criterion using a box-and-whisker plot" for displaying those written communication results: the range of scores, the mean, and the upper and lower quartile limits for each rubric criterion. Figure 5.4 illustrates the

Figure 5.1. Example of Tk20 drill-down, interactive chart showing critical thinking VALUE rubric results.

CRITICAL THINKING

Critical Thinking	# Exceeds Standard	% Exceeds Standard	# Meets Standard	% Meets Standard	# Approaches Standard	% Approaches Standard	# Developing	% Devel
Explanation of Issues	0	0%	379	56.91%	287	43.09%	0	0%
Evidence Selecting and Using information to investigate a point of view or conclusion	0	0%	142	21.32%	385	57.81%	139	20.87%
Influence of context and assumptions	63	9.46%	256	38.44%	208	31.23%	139	20.87%
Student's position (perspective, thesis/hypothesis)	63	9.46%	246	36.94%	357	53.6%	0	0%
Conclusions and related outcomes (implications and consequences)	0	0%	240	36.04%	426	63.96%	0	0%
Total/Percentage	126	3.78%	1263	37.93%	1663	49.94%	278	8.35%

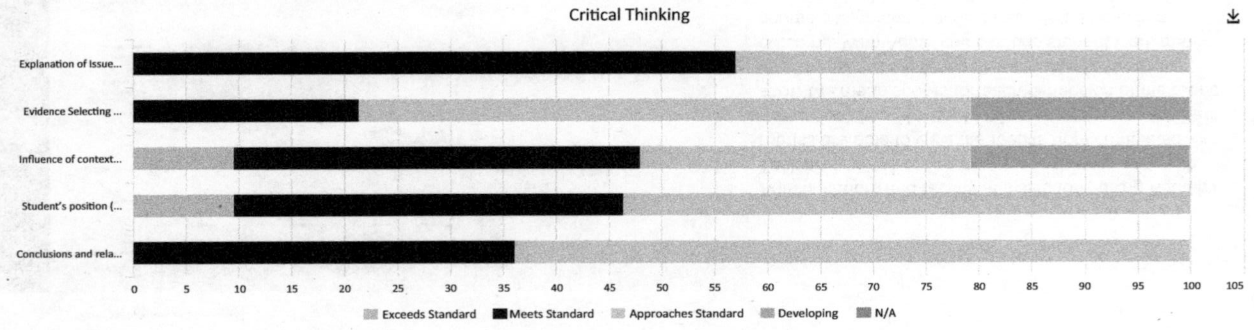

Critical Thinking

Explanation of Issue...
Evidence Selecting ...
Influence of context...
Student's position i...
Conclusions and rela...

0 5 10 15 20 25 30 35 40 45 50 55 60 65 70 75 80 85 90 95 100 105

■ Exceeds Standard   ■ Meets Standard   Approaches Standard   Developing   N/A

Source. Contributed by and used with permission from Tk20. Used with permission.

Figure 5.2. Aqua outcome performance report—summary view.

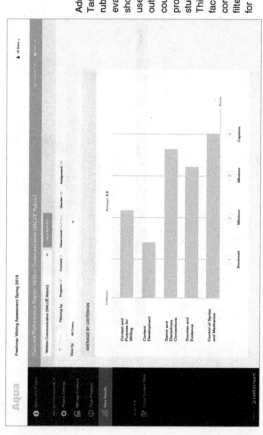

Administrators and faculty at institutions using Aqua by Taskstream™ to collect and score student work with rubrics are able to view the results from completed evaluations in real time. In this summary view, the bars show the mean scores for each dimension of the rubric used to assess student achievement of a particular outcome. With Aqua, you can use student work from course assignments across multiple courses and programs and import additional demographics about the students who produced the work for filtering the results. This example shows student performance as judged by faculty evaluators using the VALUE rubric for written communication. The results in this example have been filtered to include all assignments in five specific courses for first-year students.

Figure 5.3. Aqua outcome performance report—box-and-whisker view.

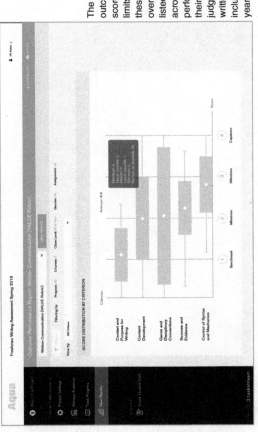

The box and whisker plot of student performance by outcome in Aqua by Taskstream™ shows the range of scores, the mean, and the upper and lower quartile limits for each rubric criterion. The specific values for these data points appear when users move the cursor over a particular criterion in the chart. The criteria are listed down the vertical axis. The numbers and labels across the horizontal axis correspond to the rubric performance levels, including the numeric scores and their labels. This example shows student performance as judged by faculty evaluators using the VALUE rubric for written communication. The results have been filtered to include all assignments in five specific courses for first-year students.

Figure 5.4. Aqua outcome performance report—single-criterion view.

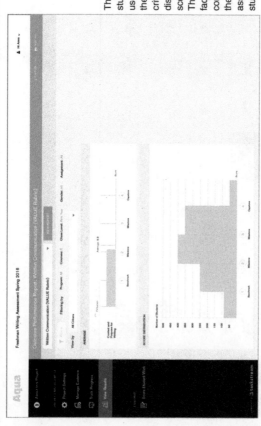

This criterion-level view in Aqua by Taskstream™ shows student performance on one dimension of the rubric used to score student work. The horizontal bar graph on the top shows the average score for the singular criterion. The bar chart below that displays the distribution of scores: the number of students who scored at each of the performance levels of the rubric. This example shows student performance as judged by faculty evaluators using the VALUE rubric for written communication. The results have been filtered to show the Context and Purpose for Writing dimension from all assignments in five specific courses for first-year students.

capacity of Aqua to display students' performance on any one criterion of the written communication rubric based on distribution of scores.

Predesigned filters built into AMSs serve multiple needs. Institution and academic leaders need to see continuously how well students across demographic lines are progressing toward achieving high-quality degree- and program-level outcomes. Faculty and others who contribute to student learning need to identify and then act on patterns of underperformance that occur midsemester or at the end of a semester to address students' equitable progress continuously. External stakeholders also need evidence of students' performance, which is documented annually as well in a commitment to real-time student assessment. There are no gaps in reporting times because the commitment is a continuous one based on each faculty member's or other contributor's posting of his or her course- or experience-based assessment results. These results serve as formative evidence of students' progress toward their summative performance levels reflected in their near-graduation work.

Adaptive Learning Platforms

Point-in-time or cycles of assessment typically untether scorers from the specific contexts in which students learn, leading to blunter recommendations for improving students' learning. Narrowing time gaps between when faculty assess and when they use their results, real-time assessment enables faculty to address on the ground the range of obstacles students face that may be related to the following kinds of variables:

- *Academic preparation or readiness.* Students may be able to memorize, for example, but unable to apply what they have memorized. Students may be able to describe a process but unable to work through it in their own practice, or they carry incorrect assumptions, concepts, or definitions that impede their ability to analyze or solve a problem.
- *Adaptation to new ways of learning and demonstrating learning.* Students may have developed successful survival study or learning strategies that previously worked and may, in fact, have been rewarded, such as memorization of material. However, these strategies may limit students' abilities to learn and use new course or program material.
- *Levels of anxiety.* Students may become immediately anxious when they learn a specific topic or subject, such as mathematics, or are required to draw on that subject in another context.
- *Points of entry.* Students are now pursuing different pathways to a degree at different points in their lives. Thus, when students

matriculate, transfer, or reenter higher education varies widely. These entry times may account for how relevant students' previous learning is or how well they draw on relevant previous learning.

However, time to identify each student's specific obstacle or set of obstacles, pressure to cover a certain amount of material in a semester or term, or class size may hinder deep inquiry into why individual students underperform. Yet, key to closing achievement gaps measurably to improve graduation rates is continuously identifying the sets of contextual challenges students face as they learn to develop on-time interventions. Though not yet at scale across the higher education landscape, the following are available: (a) adaptive learning courses or modules that adjust to meet the needs of a learner and (b) learning analytics dashboards (LADs) that display real-time data about students as they engage in a task (e.g., illustrated in Figure 5A.3).

Adaptive learning is rooted in artificial intelligence and defined as a "nonlinear approach to instruction and remediation, adjusting to a learner's interactions and demonstrated performance level and subsequently anticipating what types of content and resources learners need at a specific point in time to make progress" (Tyton Partners, 2015, p. 6). Brusilovsky (1999) identifies three distinctive components of adaptive learning platforms: "curriculum sequencing, intelligent analysis of students' solutions, and interactive problem solving support" (p. 2). These digital platforms draw on computer science, education, psychology, the science of learning, and experts in a field. Adaptive learning technology

- tailors each student's course or unit sequence based on his or her initial responses to a task or question or problem;
- flags each student's specific patterns of underperformance along his or her learning pathway;
- diagnoses the causes of those patterns, such as a missed step in solving specific kinds of problems, a misunderstanding of or confusion about terminology, or a misconception;
- branches a student to an intervention module that helps that student (a) overcome a specific pattern of underperformance, (b) practice the new learning, and (c) master that learning through built-in opportunities to rehearse it; and
- reroutes the student back into the course or unit learning sequence developed for that student.

Adaptive technology can be integrated into LMSs, such as Pearson's MyMathLab. The technology also underlies credit-bearing, online, self-paced courses or modules in some subjects such as in mathematics and statistics. Adaptive learning technology performs all of the steps listed previously based on each individual's level of learning and sets of challenges. If, for example, a student confuses the meaning of terms, the technology identifies that difficulty and routes the student to more detailed information about the terms. Following that review, the technology tests and retests the student to determine that he or she no longer confuses the terms. If a student misses a step in a procedure, again the technology flags that missed step and routes that student to related information, exercises, tests, and retests to affirm that he or she no longer misses that step.

Both face-to-face and online courses may integrate adaptive learning software into the sequencing of a course to provide students with more course content practice or to provide supplemental instruction (SI) that identifies and addresses students' patterns of weakness. Reporting features of adaptive technology platforms alert faculty or assigned tutors to the need to address student challenges so that students can progress equitably. Students also receive dashboard reports of their performance on their mobile devices so that they keep track of their performance and identify areas they need to improve. Pearson (www.pearsoned.com), McGraw-Hill Education (www.mheducation.com), Smart Sparrow (www.smartsparrow.com), and Knewton (www.knewton.com) are four providers, among others, of adaptive learning platforms for higher education.

The Bill & Melinda Gates Foundation is committed to lowering the cost of higher education, increasing access to postsecondary education, and ensuring students' achievement of quality outcomes. The foundation commissioned Education Growth Advisors (now Tyton Partners) to make the case for greatly expanding the use of adaptive learning in higher education. *Learning to Adapt: A Case for Accelerating Adaptive Learning in Higher Education* (Tyton Partners, 2015) does just that. The publication describes how adaptive learning programs individualize instruction in three different kinds of scenarios: students learning another language, students engaging in a simulation, and instructors monitoring students' progress to customize instruction in a course. It also includes a taxonomy of adaptive learning instructional models and examples of campuses that have adopted adaptive technology tools, such as Arizona State University. Sensitive to each institution's culture, the publication lists guiding questions to initiate campus discussion about using adaptive technology, such as, "What are the institution's core pedagogical values (e.g., learning styles, experiential education, competency-based assessment) and how do they align with the pedagogical values of its adaptive learning supplier?" (Tyton Partners, 2015, p. 14).

Web-Based Educational Data-Mining Tools

Web-based educational data-mining tools designed to identify institutional and student variables that affect students' performances or decisions are emerging across the landscape of higher education. The spectrum of options represented in these tools includes those that mine students' online course and educational activities data to those that mine increasingly larger databases or data-sets, such as those in student information systems (SISs) or LMSs. Used at the course level, these tools extract, report, and classify patterns related to student performance and behaviors in digital platforms. These patterns expand faculty insight into the obstacles students face as they learn.

Used at the institution level, educational data-mining tools provide a campus or system leader and administrators with new insights into the larger environmental issues or practices that affect critical institutional issues such as retention. Some tools extract data to describe existing conditions or behaviors, such as course-taking patterns. Others extract and use data to predict probable actions or consequences, such as the likelihood of students' academic success. The following two sections illustrate some examples of these tools and the contexts within which they mine data. (Resources at the end of this chapter provide in-depth descriptions of the range and specific categories of web-based educational mining tools that are available at the time of writing.)

Course- or Activity-Level Learning Analytic Tools

At one end of the spectrum of these data-mining tools are learning analytics tools that provide faculty and other contributors to student learning with real-time, data-driven insights into the sets of challenges that students face as they learn or engage in an online educational activity. Developed at the First International Conference on Learning Analytics and Knowledge in 2011, "*learning analytics* is the measurement, collection, analysis, and reporting of data about learners and their contexts, for purposes of understanding and optimizing learning and the environments in which it occurs" (Long & Siemens, 2011, p. 32). One example of a learning analytics tool is a LAD. A student LAD and an instructor LAD display evidence of students' achievement as students learn or complete a subtask of a much larger task. Instructor LADs provide data about student performance that are time-consuming to harvest in real time, particularly in large-enrollment classes. LADs also report data about what instructors do not typically see, such as the discrete kinds of actions or decisions students make while engaged in a task, the number of attempts they make to solve a problem, or their commitment to work with SI that surrounds a course. Importantly, the ways in which LAD data are reported inform faculty's real-time instructional decisions, if not during a class period, at least for the next one.

The appendix to this chapter describes educational contexts within which LADs display real-time data for students and instructors, provides examples of LAD screenshots, and focuses on the real-time assessment and instructional value of them. For example, Figure 5A.3 illustrates a dashboard display that identifies the levels at which students are performing a subtask of a larger geometry task and categorizes the specific kinds of challenges they face. Those kinds of reported real-time data inform how an instructor will help underperforming students in the next class period, enabling them to improve continuously and stay on track. By identifying patterns that thwart students' progress as they perform a task, rather than at the end of a task, LAD data narrow the time spans that typically exist between when students hand in their work and when they receive feedback. In addition, these real-time data provide evidence of students' learning and problem-solving processes that otherwise would not be visible to an instructor in students' final work.

Another genre of learning analytics is designed to predict student success, such as the likelihood of students' success in a course based on performance in previous courses. Among the kinds of predictive learning analytics tools that Dietz-Uhler and Hurn (2013) identify are the following:

- Course Signals System that issues alerts and interventions for academic issues students face;
- Progress and Course Engagement (PACE) that tracks student progress in a course, alerting faculty to the need for intervention; and
- Blackboard's Learning Content Management System that tracks student performance to predict student success. (p. 19)

Institution-Level Analytic Tools

Data-mining tools also enable leaders and administrators to answer critical institution-level questions about how the environment—such as its policies, protocols, or practices—promotes or inhibits students' timely progression toward degree completion. Requiring increasingly larger databases or data sets are mining tools designed to identify (a) institutional variables that work against students' progress or persistence, such as ineffective advising or mentoring or inconvenient course scheduling, and (b) student variables (i.e., behaviors or decisions, such as course load) that affect academic success or progress. Data extracted from these kinds of mining tools prompt immediate discussion of and decisions about new processes, practices, or protocols an institution should implement to increase students' levels of performance and persistence to graduation. Dietz-Uhler and Hurn (2013) identify institutions that have improved their policies or practices, such as retention strategies, based on what those campuses learned from the collection and analysis of institutional data. For example, the University of Alabama developed a model of retention based on mining data files of first-year students. Results of this analytics effort led the university to identify students' English course grade and total credit hours as two early indicators to track continuously (Dietz-Uhler & Hurn, 2013).

A nonprofit provider of predictive analytics, Predictive Analytics for Reporting Framework (PAR) works with two- and four-year institutions in applying predictive analytic tools to mine databases from across its member institutions to address common issues, such as retention. Rather than each institution having to bear the individual cost of launching a project to learn more about factors that affect student success, PAR leverages and reports data from its member institutions to help them jump-start efforts to address "course success, retention, and graduation rates" (PARFRAMEWORK, n.d.). The University of Maryland System represents one large-scale use of predictive analytics that is enabling the system to identify "academic points of fit between students and interventions for achieving academic success" (PARFRAMEWORK, 2015).

Though still emerging on the front line of higher education, adaptive learning and learning analytics tools will likely continue to be integrated into AMSs and LMSs such as now exist, for example, in the LMSs D2L/ Brightspace and Blackboard Analytics for Learn (A4L). Some of these technologies will also be developed as plug-ins, such as Moodle's Engagement Analytics, so that faculty and other course designers can build the tools into course content. In 2015 the instructional management system (IMS) Global Learning Consortium released its Caliper Analytics to harness student data from different online providers' courses. This platform has developed common labels to identify the activities that students engage in as they learn online, such as reading, engaging in group work, viewing a simulation, or doing an online lab. The significance of this development is that it provides online instructors with real-time data about their students' learning processes or activities, such as when and where gaps in students' learning processes occur, who is initially at risk in a course, how much time students spend accessing course content, or which digital tools students use (www.imsglobal.org/activity/caliperram). These kinds of data contribute to faculty learning about the variables that affect student achievement. Two of the first LMSs to integrate Caliper Analytics are D2L's Brightspace and Blackboard.

ePortfolios

Contributing to institution- and program-level real-time student assessment are ePortfolios. Particularly valuable are those that require students to align their authentic work along their undergraduate pathway with general education and major program-level outcomes. That alignment provides students with a view of their own progression based on faculty and other educators' consistent use of criteria and standards of judgment. For faculty, the ePortfolio is the primary source of assessment results each semester—the same results that students see. Faculty or other raters either submit their scoring results into an AMS or they may even be able to score student work online. In either case the AMS collects and then disaggregates and aggregates those results to display them visually based on the selected filters that stakeholders choose. Collaborative interrogation of end-of-semester assessment results leads to context-based interventions or practices along students' trajectory and continuously addresses students' equitable progress. In contrast, delayed-response assessment approaches or periodic assessment cycles may first involve identifying faculty volunteers who agree to submit student work samples for scoring. In real-time student assessment, ePortfolios increase access to assessment results from all courses or education experiences in a semester so that there is equal attention to how all students are performing, not a sample of them.

ePortfolios have increasingly become the medium through which faculty, other educators, and students themselves gauge progress toward achieving high-quality outcomes. Case 5.3 represents a powerful example of how studio arts faculty at Auburn University use their majors' ePortfolios to develop students' enduring and connected learning. Faculty access students' ePortfolio projects to identify work that students previously completed to position students to see "connections between and across the various courses" (p. 134, this volume) and to "experiment with strategies and processes they have used before" (p. 135, this volume). ePortfolios provide faculty with a long view of students' levels of performance, and as Case 5.3 illustrates, they provide faculty with a way to connect students to their prior learning.

Educators taking a wide view of student learning and looping students back to their previous work to maximize their learning represents an approach that can help all students make meaning of their diverse pathways, even if those pathways include credit from alternative providers or credentialing organizations. Experts on ePortfolios have already made compelling cases for the integrative value of this medium for students as well as its portability across different educational pathways, contributing to students' longitudinal view of their learning and development (see, e.g., Cambridge, 2010;

CASE 5.3.
ePortfolios as an Archive of Development in Studio Arts at Auburn University

Artists have long used portfolios to showcase their work and their artistic processes, so when Auburn University undertook an ePortfolio Project as our institution's Quality Enhancement Project, studio arts was among the first programs to join the faculty cohort. We understood the value of helping students migrate their traditional portfolios into a digital form that would be more easily shared and help students learn the website design and technology skills they would need as professional artists. We also understood the need to provide feedback as students developed the capacity to reflect on their own processes, assess their work with a trained but objective eye, and learn to exercise the critical judgment required of all artists. We worked collaboratively to closely examine our existing curriculum and make decisions about where and how students would be introduced to ePortfolios; have opportunities to reflect and receive feedback on their reflections; and, of course, produce artifacts. Actually producing artifacts is no problem for a studio arts student, but capturing clear photographs of those artifacts to document them in an ePortfolio required some consideration of both the logistics and equipment required for such photographic evidence and the curriculum that would teach students the skills they would need to create a photographic archive. We were able to quickly identify a capstone course where students would be able to assemble the final version of their ePortfolios before graduation, but it seemed important that students begin the creation of a working ePortfolio much earlier. Thus, we created a new course at the sophomore level that would get students started on the process and encourage them to archive their artistic creations and their reflective thinking about their processes and successes throughout their undergraduate studies. In addition to giving students early and frequent practice on the key skills necessary to produce a successful ePortfolio, we also saw the archive ePortfolio as useful to instructors as a record of history and development.

Studio arts students typically take a few foundational courses and then numerous courses that range from ceramics to drawing, photography to printmaking. Students take multiple pathways through the major, and so it is not uncommon for a course to enroll students the professor has never worked with alongside students the professor has taught over multiple semesters. The ePortfolio archives our students are now required to keep provide the professor with easy access to prior projects, allowing us to help students see connections between and across the various courses they take.

Students who have been working on a particular project or technique in drawing, for example, might well build on that work in a pottery class, albeit in a different medium. Students can be encouraged to experiment with strategies and processes they have used before as they work with different forms, solve new problems, or work within new constraints.

When professors look at ePortfolio archives to gather background information about a student's experience, they are not, of course, conducting formal assessments, but they are using their own experience and critical judgment to plot an action plan for fostering student growth. Consciously or not, such moments are assessments of the most immediate and valuable kind because they enable the professor to help a particular student in a particular moment to maximize his or her learning experience. What more value could we want from ePortfolios or the authentic evidence of learning they represent? What more could we ask of assessment?

Note. Contributed by Gary Wagoner, associate professor emeritus, Department of Art and Art History, Auburn University. Used with permission.

Cambridge, Cambridge, & Yancey, 2009; Chen & Light, 2010; Michelson & Mandell, 2004; Reynolds and Patten, 2015). Over the longer term, of course, if alternative providers and credentialors align their assessment of student work with the DQP/LEAP outcomes framework and existing major program outcomes frameworks, discussed in chapter 2, that learner-centered commitment would also build coherence across students' pathways. Credentialors recognize that higher education is moving toward outcomes-based frameworks and shared sets of criteria and standards of judgment. For example, in its webinar presentation to prospective students who seek credit for prior learning, *Documenting Competence: A Learning Portfolio,* the Council on Adult and Experiential Learning (CAEL) (2013) specifically points out to students that the organization is paying close attention to the outcomes-based assessment landscape in higher education. For now, what remains important for students are the following processes: (a) educators helping students see the relevance of their learning over time documented in ePortfolio work, as demonstrated in Case 5.3; and (b) students integrating their learning from other educational providers or credentialors along their education pathways.

ePortfolios are significant long-term contributors to our students' future. They provide direct evidence of what students know and can do, in contrast to grades, credit hours earned, or lists of outcomes aligned with courses or education experiences. Thus, institutions and programs that require ePortfolios can also prepare students to identify ePortfolio entries that demonstrate their applied and transferable learning for potential employers or graduate schools (see also chapter 6, Case 6.3, pp. 163–164). This preparation will become necessary given current employers' dissatisfaction with the ability of postsecondary credentialing systems to assure quality in student achievement based on grades, credit hours, or expanded course descriptions that include learning outcomes. That dissatisfaction is at the center of approximately 100 efforts now under way that are focused on determining ways to improve postsecondary credentialing. The Lumina Foundation's Connecting Credentials initiative (www.connectingcredentials.org; Lumina, 2016a) is one of those efforts. Altogether, these efforts are fueled by employers' confusion about (a) grades or other credentialing methods as accurate documentation of quality achievement and (b) the uneven ways in which student achievement is documented across postsecondary education credentialing (Lumina Foundation, 2016a, p. 9). Unfortunately, the first major update on national trends in grading in seven years, available at GradeInflation.com, does not diminish that confusion based on the widespread awarding of the "A" grade. The title of Scott Jaschik's (2016) *Inside Higher Ed* follow-up article on the update says it all: "Grade Inflation Nation: Getting an A Is Really Easier Than Ever."

If grades, then, are an unreliable representation of students' high-quality achievement, it is likely that the practice of embedding links to students' digitally stored ePortfolio work in e-transcripts may become widespread practice. That is, students' work itself, such as samples of writing or a video of a presentation, will provide concrete evidence of their achievement levels. Potential employers may also ask students to provide links to work that demonstrates, for example, their interpersonal or teamwork skills. Seeing student work will likely take precedence over seeing a list of courses or course descriptions or credits earned.

Most of the technology options presented in this chapter are evolving, even as this book goes to press. Before investing in any one of these options it is important for an institution and its programs to answer two overarching questions:

1. Can we describe how we will specifically use data that are generated from these options to improve our students' learning? Identifying how data will be used directly to inform decision making and actions to improve student learning, such as developing pedagogical strategies to help students chronologically overcome learning hurdles, is an essential first question to answer.
2. Do we have the resources and the capacity to implement and support a specific tool? (In Appendix 5, Shea, DiCerbo, and Grenier also identify

the range of institutional issues, such as features of a current educational system, that need to be addressed during initial discussions about the use of digital learning games and simulations on campus or in a program of study.)

Finally, the pace at which technology tools are developing or evolving across the landscape of higher education raises important legal, procedural, and ethical issues about the use of technology-generated data, such as the need to obtain students' consent to use personal data. In the Additional Resources section, a particular entry by Neill Sclater identifies those issues. Sclater specifies relevant examples of codes of practice for the use of learning analytics from various fields and organizations that can inform developing a code of practice in higher education.

Additional Resources

Adaptive Technology

Thompson, J. (2013). *Types of adaptive learning*. Retrieved from www .cogbooks.com/downloads/Adaptive%20Learning%20-%20Types%20 of%20Adaptive%20Learning.pdf

For the novice, this white paper provides an introduction to the major types of adaptive technologies that currently exist.

Tyton Partners. (2013). *Learning to adapt: Understanding the adaptive learning supplier landscape*. Education Growth Advisors, now Tyton Partners. Retrieved from tytonpartners.com/tyton-wp/wp-content/uploads/2015/01/ Learning-to-Adapt_Supplier-Landscape.pdf

This document provides institutional stakeholders with frameworks and resources to initiate campus discussions about evaluation and adoption of adaptive learning options. The author points out that a decision to purchase adaptive technology tools (many of which are described in the publication) should not be based initially on the capacity of an individual vendor. Rather, the decision should be based first on users' needs and then on considerations of institutional capacity to implement an option. This resource is updated periodically.

AMSs

Oakleaf, M., Belander, J., & Carlie Graham, C. (2013, April). *Choosing and using assessment management systems: What librarians need to know*. Association of College and Research Libraries. Conference Paper. Retrieved from www .ala.org/acrl/sites/ala.org.acrl/files/content/conferences/confsandpreconfs/ 2013/papers/OakleafBelangerGraham_Choosing.pdf

This resource provides all stakeholders with helpful descriptions of and comparisons among the leading AMSs that enable stakeholders to identify capacities they need to improve assessment efforts. As the authors wisely state, these systems evolve rapidly; thus, it is necessary to check with each vendor about developments. Capacities of systems are compared in an assessment management chart based on the following characteristics:

- assessment ability
- outcomes alignment
- repository capacity
- data management
- system integration
- support services
- internal reporting/accreditation reporting
- action taking (supports closing the loop processes, reporting of data to stakeholders, generating assessment plans, and action plans)

ePortfolio Providers

Batson, T. (2011, October 12). A survey of the electronic portfolio market sector: Analysis and surprising trends. *About Campus*. Retrieved from campustechnology.com/articles/2011/10/12/a-survey-of-the-electronic-portfolio-market-sector.aspx

The author provides an annotated list of ePortfolio technology providers, remarking on the growth of this market since the list was compiled in 2007, the incorporation of rubrics into ePortfolio technology, and the wider use of them to score student work from a range of learning experiences besides formal coursework.

Lorenzo, G., & Ittelson, J. (2005, July). *An overview of e-portfolios*. Educause Learning Initiative. Paper 1. Retrieved from net.educause.edu/ir/library/pdf/ELI3001.pdf

Along with reviewing ePortfolio technology, this report defines and categorizes *ePortfolios*, illustrates how some institutions have implemented them, and addresses adoption issues.

LMSs

McIntosh, D. (2015). *Vendors of learning management and e-learning products*. Trimeritus eLearning Solutions. Retrieved from www.trimeritus.com/vendors.pdf

This resource provides institutional stakeholders with a comprehensive current list of vendors along with brief descriptions of each platform.

This resource is periodically updated. Categories of providers include the following:

- corporate LMSs
- learning content management systems (LCMSs)
- course authoring tools
- virtual classrooms
- generic courseware
- education LMSs (ELMSs)

Web-Based Educational Data-Mining Tools

Czerkawaski, B. C. (2015, Spring). When learning analytics meets e-learning. *Online Journal of Distance Learning Administration, 18*(2). University of West Georgia, Distance Education Center. Retrieved from www.westga .edu/~distance/ojdla/summer182/czerkawski182.html

The author provides a helpful overview of the various purposes of learning analytics, primarily in e-learning. Within that context he identifies (a) higher education projects in learning analytics, such as those at the University of Michigan; (b) advantages and concerns related to using analytic tools; and (c) different techniques used in this educational technology.

Dietz-Uhler, B., & Hurn, J. E. (2013, Spring). Using learning analytics to predict (and improve) student success: A faculty perspective. *Journal of Interactive Online Learning, 12*(1): 17–26. Retrieved from www.ncolr.org/jiol/ issues/pdf/12.1.2.pdf

Authors discuss how faculty can use learning analytics in their courses to predict and improve student success as well as to request academic resources based on data-based evidence provided by learning analytics tools. They also identify institutions using learning analytics tools; types of data that analytics tools mine; and the uses and benefits of analytics tools at the course, program, institution, and even national levels.

Educause Analytics and Higher Education Library. (2015). Retrieved from www.educause.edu/ library/resources/analytics-higher-education-2015

Educause's online library houses reports and supporting materials on analytics such as current landscape reports, institutional analytics reports, surveys, data tables, and institutional slide presentations. These resources help institutions understand current and future directions of analytics and provide guidance to those who want to develop analytics programs.

Huebner, R. A. (2013, April). A survey of educational data mining research. *Research in Higher Education Journal, 19*, 1–13.

The author presents a survey of data mining research specifically focused on educational data mining tools aimed at improving institutional effectiveness and student learning. The article begins with a brief history of data mining and its usefulness in identifying patterns in large data sets. It then identifies research that describes how specific data mining tools are now being used to analyze data to address questions about student retention and attrition, to identify and adapt to students learning needs, and to predict student performance in online learning environments through analysis of course management system data.

Sclater, N. (2014). *Code of practice for learning analytics: A literature review of the ethical and legal issues.* Joint Information Systems Committee (JISC), United Kingdom. Retrieved from repository.jisc.ac.uk/5661/1/Learning_Analytics_A_ Literature_Review.pdf

The author identifies major ethical, procedural, and legal issues related to implementing learning analytics tools such as ownership of data, privacy issues, and data sharing. He also identifies relevant codes of practice in various fields and organizations that can inform developing a code of practice in higher education.

"All Play Means Something": Using Digital Learning Games and Simulations to Support Instructional Planning and Assessment

Play is more than a mere physiological phenomenon or a psychological reflex. It goes beyond the confines of a purely physical or purely biological activity. It is a significant function—that is to say, there is some sense to it. In play there is something "at play" which transcends the immediate needs of life and imparts meaning to the action. All play means something.

—Johan Huizinga, *Homo Ludens: A Study of the Play-Element in Culture* (1995, p. 1)

U ntil the mid-twentieth century, simulation technology was often complex and expensive. The emergence of personal computing in the final quarter of the last century made it possible to create virtual worlds in a digital environment. Among the most promising developments in instructional technology over the past few decades are the emergence of learning simulations (sometimes referred to as *sims*) and digital games for learning (often referred to as *serious games*). Sims and serious games for learning are "highly interactive virtual environments" (Aldrich, 2009a, p. 4) that promote learning outcomes by providing a student player or group of players with serious challenges within a virtual environment. At the same time they gather students' performance data. There is a similarity between games and sims: both are set in an "interactive environment in which features in the environment behave similarly to real-world events" (Clark & Mayer, 2003, p. 468). However, games are often distinguished from sims by the traditional requirements of gameplay—competition and the assignment of points necessary to bring about a win-or-lose outcome. Also, as Aldrich (2009b) points out, "Compared to educational simulations, serious games tend to be more fun" (p. 7). Well-designed games/simulations provide learners with cognitive challenges that promote learning while collecting and generating data on student performance that can be used for instructional planning and assessment. How these tools contribute to instructional planning and assessment is the focus of this appendix.

The Capacity of Games/Simulations to Collect Real-Time, In-Depth Data About Student Performance Variables

In many games/sims, the capacity to collect in-depth information about player/student performance variables creates key assessment data for faculty and students. Data from gameplay are displayed for the player/student and the instructor in a learning analytics dashboard (LAD). LADs are data aggregation tools that display student performance statistics. Learning management systems (LMSs) such as Blackboard or Canvas also can aggregate and display statistical data on student behavior and performance. LADs found in LMSs tend to track information such as frequency of student login attempts, quiz/online test scores, the number of discussion posts a student submits, and whether a student has uploaded an assignment. The assessment value of these data is limited. Frequently, the most important student work is completed outside the LMS, such as in a written assignment or in mathematics computations. The analytics tools in a standard LMS can record when such work is submitted for an instructor's review. It cannot assess the quality of the student's work or the student's progress toward the course's learning outcomes.

LADs in games/simulations are qualitatively different from those found in LMSs and other forms of educational software in that the major instructional event or experience takes place within the serious game/simulation instead of in a physical classroom or offline. Consequently, the LAD in a game/simulation can track and record more forms of and a greater variety of relevant data on student actions and decisions than LADs attached to more conventional educational software. Examples of data that can be tracked in a game/sim include

- time it takes to solve a problem,
- strategies a player employs to solve a problem,
- varieties and types of errors a player makes when problem-solving,
- ability to solve problems in cooperation with others, and
- types of problems that a player finds easy or difficult to solve.

These new forms of student data collection contribute to a more robust and diverse approach to instructional planning and student performance assessment than previously possible. In short, they enable faculty and researchers to look closely at the decisions students make in the course of an instructional task or challenge, providing heretofore invisible data about the challenges they face. In addition, these data can influence faculty and instructional designers' decisions about course design.

Examples of LAD Data for Faculty and Students in Simulations and Games

Simformer and Agent Surefire

Examples of simulation reports generated by a simulation software product, Simformer, and a game, *Agent Surefire*, illustrate some of the kinds of data that can be displayed on LADs for students and faculty. Simformer is a simulation software product designed to introduce students to decision-making in a global business environment. It "simulates processes and trends taking place today in retail, manufacturing, global trade, services, mining, agriculture, and even medicine and science" (Simformer, n.d.). Simformer offers a learning management system that provides instructors with data on student performance in the simulation and students with data on their performance of tasks, enabling them to track the success of their virtual business. Figure A5.1 is a screenshot that provides an instructor with data about a student's financial performance.

Agent Surefire is a game intended to train players to think critically about cybersecurity issues. Players adopt the role of Agent Surefire, a cybersecurity expert tasked with finding an employee within a company who is stealing trade secrets and sharing them with a criminal hacker. As players make their way through the game, several challenges are presented that relate to skills needed for cybersecurity work, such as recognizing that a worker's carelessness with confidential information can jeopardize security. Points are assigned based, for example, on how successful students are in examining a worker's desk and then properly identifying the category of an identified threat. At the end of the gameplay, students see how well they have performed on their LAD, illustrated in Figure A5.2.

Insight Learning System

Working with teachers to determine the kinds of data they need to learn about the specific sets of challenges third-grade students encounter as they learn how to measure area, a group at Pearson worked with teachers to develop the LAD for its Insight Learning System. This system integrates digital games, digital tasks, and in-person activities. A major challenge of digital learning environments is that when students are engaged with them, teachers actually see less work product than they do when grading traditional paper-and-pencil activities. LADs must provide sufficient information to make up for this lack of teacher information. Based on several design versions presented to teachers, the LAD for the Insight project was designed to do the following:

Figure A5.1. Simformer instructor LAD screenshot.

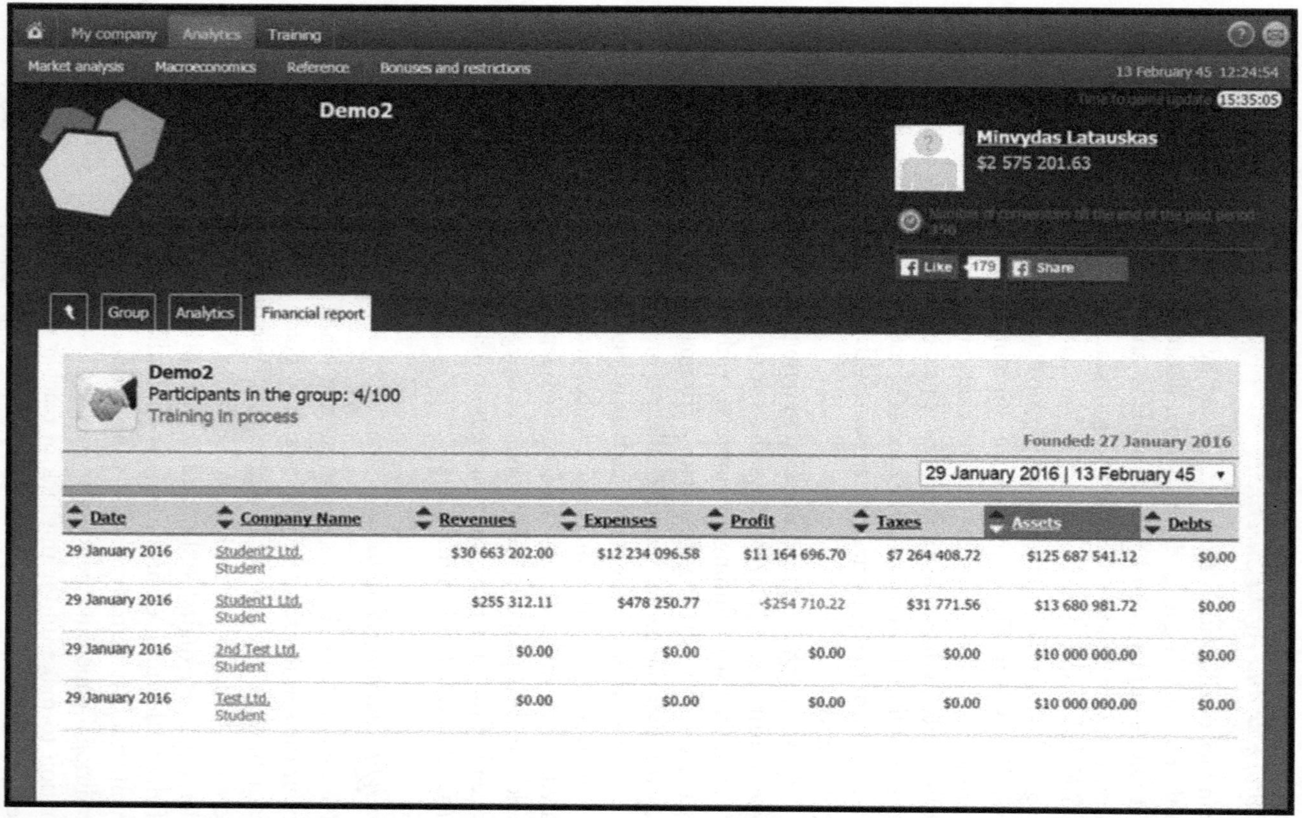

Source. Simformer.com. Reprinted with permissions.

Figure A5.2. *Agent Surefire* student LAD screenshot.

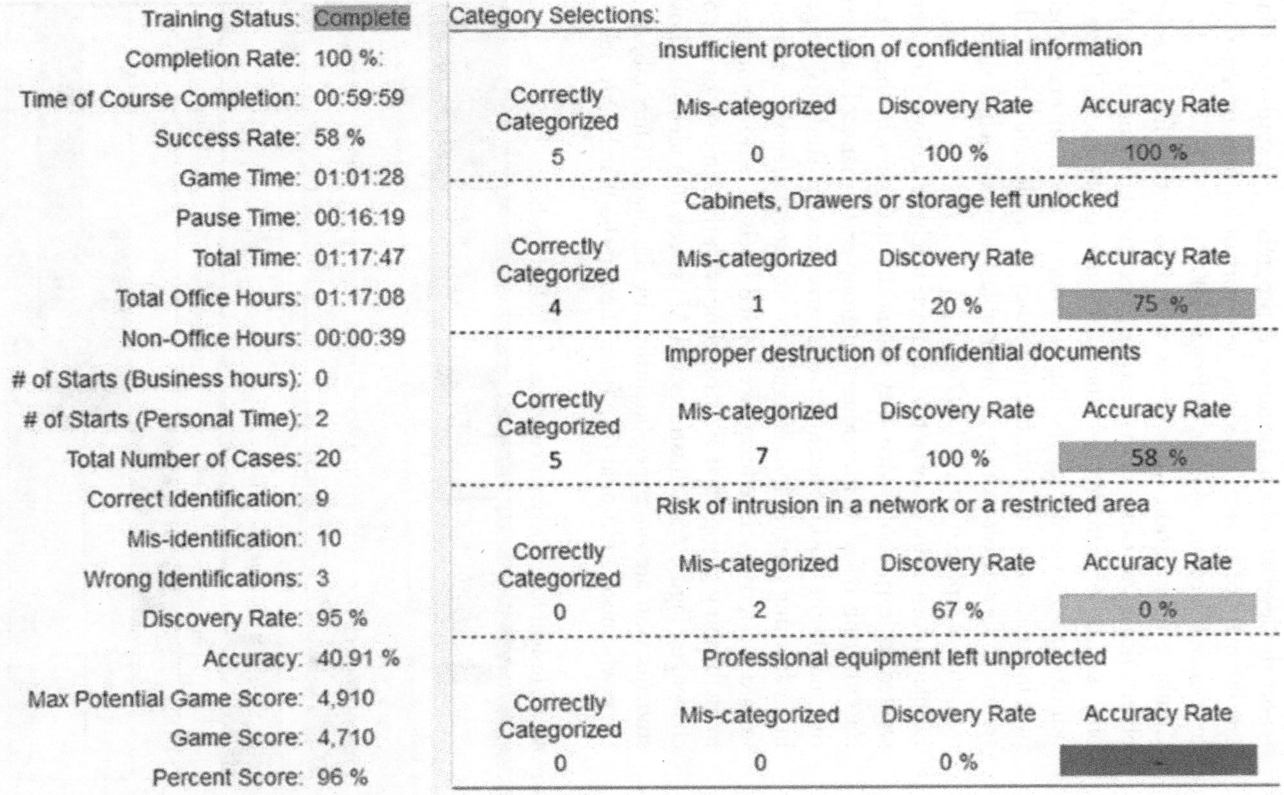

Training Status:	Complete
Completion Rate:	100 %:
Time of Course Completion:	00:59:59
Success Rate:	58 %
Game Time:	01:01:28
Pause Time:	00:16:19
Total Time:	01:17:47
Total Office Hours:	01:17:08
Non-Office Hours:	00:00:39
# of Starts (Business hours):	0
# of Starts (Personal Time):	2
Total Number of Cases:	20
Correct Identification:	9
Mis-Identification:	10
Wrong Identifications:	3
Discovery Rate:	95 %
Accuracy:	40.91 %
Max Potential Game Score:	4,910
Game Score:	4,710
Percent Score:	96 %

Category Selections:

Insufficient protection of confidential information

Correctly Categorized	Mis-categorized	Discovery Rate	Accuracy Rate
5	0	100 %	100 %

Cabinets, Drawers or storage left unlocked

Correctly Categorized	Mis-categorized	Discovery Rate	Accuracy Rate
4	1	20 %	75 %

Improper destruction of confidential documents

Correctly Categorized	Mis-categorized	Discovery Rate	Accuracy Rate
5	7	100 %	58 %

Risk of intrusion in a network or a restricted area

Correctly Categorized	Mis-categorized	Discovery Rate	Accuracy Rate
0	2	67 %	0 %

Professional equipment left unprotected

Correctly Categorized	Mis-categorized	Discovery Rate	Accuracy Rate
0	0	0 %	-

Source. MAVI Interactive, LLC. Reprinted with permission.

- Provide information at the right level of specificity to be helpful for teachers. To achieve this need, for example, the dashboard is able to report the level at which a student is progressing toward mastering measurement of an area, based on the theory of learning progressions in science (Cocoran, Mosher, & Rogat, 2009).
- Combine information from games with information from teacher observations and other digital activity, because the game is not the only source of information about student proficiency. Teachers wanted to see evidence of specific behaviors rather than make their own inferences about students' proficiency. To achieve that need, the system applies direct scoring to observable evidence, such as time on task, that is reported on the LAD.
- Display information in a way that supports teacher decisions. Teachers wanted to learn about what they should do or review in their next class meeting, based on individual and group performance. To achieve that need, the LAD presents a class overview of students' stages in the learning progression, designed to monitor students' movement toward mastery-level performance. Mixed levels of performance lead to establishing groups that are struggling with the same set or sets of challenges. Figure A5.3 illustrates an LAD screen that identifies those students who are on target (identified in the Shout Outs tab) and those who need additional help (identified in the Watch Outs tab).

Figure A5.3. Insight learning system instructor LAD screenshot.

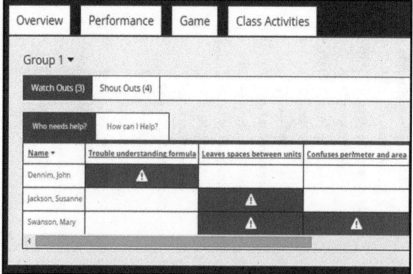

Source. Contributed by Kristen DiCerbo, vice president, education research, Pearson. Used with permission.

Challenges Related to Adopting Games and Simulations

Despite the demonstrated potential of games and simulations as tools for instruction and assessment and the fact that games and simulations for learning have a long history, there has not been, as yet, widespread adoption of their use in formal education settings. Along with cost, researchers have identified several challenges that institutions face in adopting games and simulations: implementation, actual use of the technology in terms of classroom management and the time it takes to play games, features of a current educational system, and the absence of clear guidelines and best practices for integrating games and simulations in the formal classroom setting (Watson, Yang, & Ruggiero, 2013). Multiple studies have also indicated that a lack of alignment between games and learning objectives/standards and an inability to track student progress or evaluate learning performance also challenge implementation of games and simulations (Justice & Ritzhaupt, 2015; Watson et al., 2013).

Challenges using technology often involve issues of older hardware that cannot cope with demands for heavy graphics and issues with networks that are not able to carry the data loads from games. Issues related to adoption include the cost of games and simulations. Computer-based games and simulations are a form of instructional technology and, as such, need to be factored into an institution's instructional technology budget. Educational institutions have an understandable aversion to incurring new costs for technology that does not yet have an extensive record of documented success in schools and colleges. There is grant funding to support the piloting of educational innovations. The Bill & Melinda Gates Foundation has emerged in recent years as a resource to promote innovation in schools and colleges. For postsecondary institutions, grants from the Fund for the Improvement of Postsecondary Education (FIPSE) of the U.S. Department of Education have been another source that supports piloting innovative programs and learning technologies.

Institutional resistance to a mode of learning that does not fit easily into traditional educational paradigms may also challenge adopting games and sims. Many faculty and school/college administrators lack a clear understanding of how to integrate games/simulations into their existing curriculum (Watson et al., 2013). This problem is particularly acute for faculty and staff who are wedded to older instructional paradigms that emphasize content delivery with faculty instructors who function primarily as a sage on the stage or who are reluctant to change (Goffe & Kauper, 2014; Reilly, 2015). In those cases, instructional time spent running simulations or "playing games" may be perceived as detracting from—rather than adding to—achieving the learning objectives of the course. Further, there is the additional responsibility for faculty to train their students in the use of these tools—especially students who may themselves be uncomfortable learning new technologies and who may also be invested in the traditional instructional paradigm (in which they often play a passive role while content is delivered). Finally, simulations and games do not produce traditional student artifacts: there is less visible student work than in the case of traditional assessment artifacts (e.g., paper-based exams and quizzes, term papers, class presentations) that have a physical presence. Other challenges that result from the current educational system include lack of supporting materials and lesson plans for integrating games, lack of professional development, and pressures of a standards-based assessment environment (Watson et al., 2013).

Reconciling games and simulations with a traditional educational paradigm is a significant obstacle. However, in the end, what may overcome both the cost issues and institutional reluctance to implement games and simulations are the following instructional needs: (a) a greater amount and more varieties of student data and different types of student performance data that are more detailed and varied than what is produced by traditional student work and (b) displays of data to inform student performance evaluation and instructional design and decision-making. In addition, the push for more active learning approaches (as opposed to passive content delivery) and the comfort level of students with digital technology may also play a major role in the adoption of games and simulations. The digital era provides us new opportunities to gather data about student actions.

While data by themselves do not have meaning, with careful design they can be turned into evidence of student proficiency (DiCerbo & Behrens, 2014). Well-designed games and simulations allow us to capture evidence not only of students' final answers but also the processes they took to reach them. Using these new tools wisely, we can greatly enhance the quality of educational assessment and instructional decisions, leading to an improvement in the achievement of learning outcomes for students. We can create a rich portrait of strengths, weaknesses, and progress. Essentially, we can have assessment without tests. To reach this potential, we need ways to make visible the evidence from games and simulations and to support the decisions for which we design the assessments. Thoughtful LAD creation can help us close the loop from data to information.

Further Information

This appendix was contributed by Peter Shea, director, Office of Professional Development, Middlesex Community College; Kristen DiCerbo, principal research scientist and lead of the Center for Learning Science and Technology at Pearson; and Jim Grenier, director of online education, Mass Bay Community College. It is used with permission.

This appendix was developed specifically for this book to enhance readers' understanding of how digital games and simulations are being used to provide (a) students with opportunities to apply their learning and (b) faculty and students simultaneously with data about student performance in real time. A full version of this paper, including the research behind Pearson's development of a geometry simulation that provides teachers with real-time evidence of each student's learning process, is available on Peter Shea's website (www.middlesex.mass.edu/RLOs/839/APMS.pdf).

APPROACHES TO TAKING
REAL-TIME STUDENT
ASSESSMENT TO SCALE

Taking real-time student assessment to scale in programs, let alone at the institution level, may send anxiety through the hearts of many, not to mention trigger immediate objections such as, "It takes too much time," "That only works for specialized or nationally accredited programs," or "Our enrollments are too large to adjust to this kind of commitment." Yet faculty teaching in some specialized and nationally accredited programs—regardless of the size of their student populations—sustain a real-time student assessment commitment, remaining focused on their students' progress toward achieving stated performance expectations for students' near-graduation-level work. Understandably, however, recalibrating a currently entrenched assessment process may well meet opposition. To help institutions and programs make this commitment, in this chapter I identify some initiatives that pave the way toward building a comprehensive real-time assessment commitment to benefit all currently enrolled students. Case studies illustrate how four universities have launched campus-based initiatives to prepare more faculty and other contributors to student learning to engage collaboratively in real-time student assessment.

Initial Approaches

Institutions and programs can take some initial approaches to pave the way toward widening a commitment to real-time assessment. These approaches are particularly worthwhile first steps for institutions that believe their student enrollment is too large to undertake this commitment. These targeted early efforts position colleagues to see the value of moving from real-time assessment results to on-the-ground-interventions that improve students' learning.

Identify High-Risk Courses or Modules That Stretch Across Students' Degree Pathways, From Point of Matriculation, Transfer, or Reentry Into Higher Education to Point of Graduation

Early on, courses in writing or mathematics are likely among those considered to be high risk. Many first-year students fail those courses or may pass them but continue to struggle to improve their abilities over time, thus necessitating continued monitoring of their future performance. There are also high-risk courses in students' major programs of study, such as statistics or disciplinary or professional courses that integrate quantitative reasoning and build on students' earlier learning. If that earlier learning is weak, students will struggle as they progress. Sharing demographically disaggregated real-time assessment results with colleagues and other campus professionals triggers discussion about ways to address students' patterns of underperformance in the short and long term. Succumbing to inevitable failure rates in high-risk courses without timely and longitudinal interventions undermines the possibility of students' development over time. As the faculty in the Occupational Therapy Program at Salem State University do, identifying the specific strengths and weaknesses of incoming students through early assessments is the baseline upon which to report regularly students' chronological performance levels against high-quality expectations (chapter 4, pp. 107–108).

Identify High-Risk Learning Outcomes

Faculty and other contributors to student learning at the institution and program levels need to identify (a) the outcomes that are typically difficult for students to achieve at high-quality levels, such as critical thinking, writing, quantitative reasoning, and problem-solving, or (b) specific attributes of those outcomes that challenge students, such as the ability to synthesize or examine the assumptions of others. One way to determine those high-risk outcomes is to ask faculty, other education professionals, and those who support student learning in academic and student support services to identify underperformance patterns they regularly see in students' authentic work or behaviors. What patterns of underperformance do experts in the writing center, for example, see as students progress in their studies? What kinds of challenges do librarians find themselves repeatedly addressing as students progress? Asking faculty to identify areas of underperformance they see in students' near-graduation work is another strategy, providing faculty and other contributors to student learning in each program with a shared focus for a real-time assessment process.

Initially Reduce Intervals of Time Between Current Assessment Reporting Times to Connect Results With On-the-Ground Actions to Improve Currently Enrolled Students' Learning

The longer the time between assessment cycles, the greater the possibility that students who are the most vulnerable will remain invisible or that their patterns of underperformance will not be addressed in time to improve those students' learning. Focusing on students' equitable progress requires closing gaps that currently exist between assessment cycles or point-in-time assessment approaches. Closing gaps enables educators to address learners' needs as they continue to transfer, apply, and integrate their outcomes in different and increasingly more complex contexts. This longitudinal commitment promotes enduring learning.

Identify and Then Track the Most Vulnerable Cohorts of Students

Knowing the demographic composition of a student body, such as described in chapter 1, as well as students' levels of academic preparation, enables an institution and its programs to identify the most vulnerable cohorts that initially need to be monitored closely. Nonnative speakers, students who are more narrowly prepared academically, students with disabilities, nontraditional-age students, first-generation students, and students from low-income families represent initial cohorts to monitor semester-by-semester or even at midsemester.

Initially Assess Students' Near-Graduation Work to Identify Patterns of Underperformance That Need to Be Addressed Longitudinally

Although assessing students' near-graduation work typically does not benefit graduating students or even other enrolled students—unless interventions are implemented on time—this initial focus does make the case for undertaking a longitudinal commitment to assessing students' learning based on those near-graduation results. Those final results identify patterns of underperformance that need to be addressed across the general education program and each program of study so that students develop high-quality outcomes over time and internalize what high quality looks like. This approach, then, sensitizes faculty and other contributors to student learning to the value of a shared longitudinal commitment to real-time assessment.

Learn How Colleagues in Specialized or Nationally Accredited Programs Continuously Assess Their Students' Progress and Use Results to Advance Currently Enrolled Students

Across institutions there are colleagues who closely monitor their students' progress based on their specialized or national accreditation standards, as Salem State University's Occupational Therapy Program illustrates (see pp. 107–109). Thus, these colleagues offer models for other programs to adapt or adopt, including assessing students' progress toward achieving high-quality general education outcomes beyond courses in the institution's general education program of study.

Four Case Studies: Initiatives to Advance Real-Time Student Assessment

Reflecting the pressing need to ensure that currently enrolled students are equitably achieving program- and degree-level high-quality outcomes, the following institutions have initiated and continue to build on campus-based projects or practices that lead to a shared institutional commitment to real-time assessment. Their cases demonstrate different approaches that campuses have used or are using to increasingly engage more faculty and other contributors to the success of currently enrolled students.

The University of Nebraska–Lincoln

Identifying collaboration within a respectful setting as key to advancing real-time assessment, administrators at the University of Nebraska–Lincoln (UNL) launched a yearlong faculty inquiry project, partnering university administrators and faculty from across its eight undergraduate colleges. This initiative drew together faculty from across disciplines to develop disciplinary tools to assess the university's Achievement-Centered Education (ACE) general education courses and agree on shared rubrics to assess students' authentic disciplinary work representing the shared outcomes of those courses. As Case 6.1 describes, developing a community of practice generated cross-disciplinary discussion about students' performance of shared outcomes and ways to improve patterns of underperformance in students' major programs of study. These discussions also generated related strands of inquiry about the curricular design and sequencing that develop currently enrolled students' expected levels of performance and about faculty opportunities to monitor students' real-time progress toward expected levels of performance beyond achievement in a single course.

CASE 6.1.
University of Nebraska-Lincoln: Faculty Inquiry Project

Key to successfully engaging faculty in the assessment process is helping them find meaning in their work. At a large institution, such as the University of Nebraska-Lincoln (UNL) with its Achievement-Centered Education (ACE) general education program built around 10 student learning outcomes, the task is daunting. To address this need, the ACE 10 Inquiry Project was created to involve faculty in identifying and sharing best practices for assessing the ACE 10 outcome, which requires students to generate a creative or scholarly product via integrative learning. In particular, this project aimed to help faculty engage in conversations about ACE 10 assessment, develop tools for assessing ACE 10 courses that could be implemented immediately, and explore the feasibility of shared rubrics for assessing student performance in ACE 10 courses across disciplines.

In the 2013–2014 school year, 26 faculty from UNL's eight undergraduate colleges met monthly to explore methods for assessing work produced in ACE 10 courses and participate in a collegial community to address the following questions:

- How does your analysis of collected student work from ACE 10 courses demonstrate that students are meeting the outcome?
- What does your analysis of students' work tell you about how students are prepared more generally within your degree program?
- What best practices and structures for ACE 10 assessment could be shared across units for the improvement of teaching and learning?

Participants showcased the results of their assessments via posters at the campus research fair and posts on university websites. Their findings were also cycled back into individual department discussions about ACE 10 courses and undergraduate major assessment more broadly. A brochure titled *Learning from ACE Assessment: 2014 Update* was also distributed to over 1,300 UNL faculty, spotlighting how ACE assessment has supported improvements in teaching and learning.[1]

Faculty observations reflect the insights they gained and weaknesses they could address from assessing student work. For instance, English faculty discovered that assessment inspires new questions about student learning, as one member of the faculty described:

Within the composition program, we learned how much teachers benefit from the opportunity to reflect on student work across courses—that is, to see beyond the individual classroom. While our data indicate that most of our students are performing at a proficient level, our collective reading of three years' worth of portfolios showed us that their experiences in composition classes are often quite different from section to section. We wondered whether students might benefit from more shared experiences in their courses; this reminded us that assessment not only answers questions but sparks new ones. We want them to understand that teaching and learning are iterative processes requiring ongoing reflection and revision.

—Shari Stenberg, English

A postsurvey of participants (Table 6.1.1) showed that they strongly benefitted from the project, agreeing or strongly agreeing with the following statements:

TABLE 6.1.1
Postsurvey Assessment Project Results

Statement	Percent (%) Agree or Strongly Agree
I explored methods and tools for assessing work produced in ACE 10 courses.	86.7
I developed a collegial community for sharing ideas about ACE 10 curriculum and assessment.	100
I learned about AAC&U's VALUE rubrics for assessing student learning.	80
I learned strategies to connect ACE 10 assessment to department curricular discussions.	86.7
I developed a process for creating my unit's ACE 10 assessment report.	86.7
I found my participation in the ACE 10 Project a valuable experience.	93.3
I would recommend a similar ACE-focused project to my colleagues.	93.3

Confirming what other researchers have learned as the most cited reason for improving assessment (Rodgers, Grays, Fulcher, & Jurich, 2012), participants in this study said they appreciated the opportunity to consult with someone about assessment. Faculty commented most positively on the opportunity to share insights with colleagues about assessment. In response to the question, "What did you find most useful about your participation in this project," one wrote, "Hearing about other ACE 10 courses across campus and talking with faculty about their strategies for delivering and assessing them. Learning more about assessment tools. Generally, getting some inspiration to make improvements to my ACE 10 course." Another responded, "Meeting and listening to faculty from diverse programs and learning about their approaches to ACE 10 assessment."

Faculty also used the process to identify areas for improving student achievement within particular courses. For example, students majoring in advertising and public relations complete one of three capstone courses to develop an integrated marketing communications campaign for a real client. Faculty evaluated final projects using the National Institute for Learning Outcomes Assessment and the Association of American Colleges & Universities' (AAC&U) Valid Assessment of Learning in Undergraduate Education (VALUE) rubric. Results indicated that, overall, students demonstrated proficiency in broad knowledge, technical proficiency, information collection and synthesis, interpretation, and presentation. However, faculty noticed deficiencies in writing and secondary and primary research for strategy formation. The department revised an existing strategy course to emphasize research earlier in the curriculum and developed a new required course in strategic writing.

The Faculty Inquiry Project served as a model for other faculty teaching ACE 10 courses when they submitted their assessment reports the following year. The effort appears to have been beneficial. Institutionally, an analysis of ACE 10 assessment reports revealed a general sense of satisfaction with the level of student accomplishment, with the exception of two weaknesses detected in writing and research skills. The university-wide Assessment Committee is now initiating discussions regarding these concerns.

As organizers of this project, we learned the following about assessing student outcomes on our campus:[2]

- Developing communities of practice among the faculty across disciplines helped gain new ideas for implementation in their own departments.
- Even among faculty leaders, the level of understanding about assessment practices differed. The project offered a good way to help educate each other in a respectful setting and expanded the notion of assessment leadership to include faculty leaders as well as administrators.
- Follow-up analysis showed that participants in this project valued sharing ideas across disciplines to improve student learning. For instance, some faculty appreciated learning about how their

colleagues use "learning letters" to help students reflect on their learning. Seeing evidence of how students represent their own learning development helped faculty identify areas for curricular improvement.

- Faculty members participating in this project demonstrated that they gained a better understanding of the many uses of assessment. Sometimes the data inspired faculty to ask questions about the major, such as, "Where in the curriculum are students having opportunities to write within their discipline?" or "How do students demonstrate throughout the courses in their major that they can incorporate primary research?" Faculty in the project not only understood better how to assess their ACE 10 courses and the role of the course in the major, but also learned the pressing needs to participate in assessment for institutional and professional accreditation.
- Faculty expressed a desire for standardized and simplified assessment tools that could streamline their workload and provide more information about how their students' learning compared to students in other ACE courses across the university.

Partnering faculty and administrators in this assessment project proved beneficial for all. Administrators learned how they could help faculty create more meaningful assessment of student achievement and faculty expanded their understanding of how exchanging ideas about assessment could improve student learning.

Notes
1. Available at ace.unl.edu/assessment/learningfromACEassessment
2. For more information, see Guetterman & Mitchell (2015)

Note. Contributed by Amy Goodburn, associate vice chancellor, and Nancy Mitchell, director of undergraduate programs, University of Nebraska–Lincoln. Used with permission.

As the authors of this case study state, creating time and opportunities for faculty to exchange ideas about assessment harnessed others' expertise and assessment practices. Equally as important, this yearlong project surfaced the importance of monitoring students' real-time achievement levels beyond a single course. Students' learning letters reflecting their real-time progress in writing and the English department's practice of self-reflecting on students' writing across courses—to see beyond the classroom—illustrate the value of real-time assessment for currently enrolled students as well as for faculty.

Governors State University

Based on its traditionally underserved student population, Governors State University (GSU) recently launched an initiative in collaboration with others in its professional campus network to identify and address the academic as well as personal needs of its first-year students. Documented in Case 6.2, these fine-tuned coordinated efforts were aimed at keeping students on track by closely monitoring their progress on many fronts. Included among those efforts were reporting students' mid-semester academic performance in thematic linked cohort general education courses, addressing students' academic gaps with on-time interventions and support workshops, incorporating peer mentors and student success teams that consist of individuals from the institution's network of professionals, and developing intrusive advising. The efficacy of this initiative—illustrating individuals' resilience in gauging and responding to student challenges as they arise—has now led to expanding this real-time collaborative approach to all students in their second year.

CASE 6.2.
Governors State University: Targeted Student Success and Persistence Efforts for First-Year Students

Background Information

Governors State University (GSU) implemented a comprehensive new plan for general education in the fall semester of 2014, which involved students in learning communities, first-year seminars, common intellectual experiences, and writing-intensive courses. These practices are four of the high-impact practices espoused by the Association of American Colleges & Universities (AAC&U) as benefiting traditionally underserved students. Student learning outcomes guide the program, which was developed in concert with recommendations from the AAC&U's Liberal Education and America's Promise (LEAP) and Lumina's Degree Qualifications Profile (DQP) for undergraduates. The outcomes encompass learning in the areas of foundational knowledge, practical skills, social responsibility, and integrative learning. These outcomes clearly articulate the expectations for students and formed the basis for course and curriculum development.

The general education curriculum features three required, linked cohort courses per semester during the first three semesters. The cohort courses are taught by full-time faculty in groups of no more than 30 students, except for the writing courses, which are capped at 15 students.

These courses are organized around three thematic areas—civic engagement, global citizenship, and sustainability. Students stay in the same theme area for three semesters and have courses with the same group of students during that time. Faculty coordinate shared readings and assignments that build on the theme. Extracurricular activities also use the themes. This scheduling guarantees each student a seat in the required courses and takes the guesswork out of which course meets the general education requirements. It allows students to get to know each other and the faculty in smaller groups and permits exploration of different disciplines early in the college experience. At the end of those three semesters, students complete all their general education courses for communication, humanities and fine arts, and social and behavioral sciences in the cohort. Students also take one to two courses per semester outside the cohort to meet the requirements in math and science. The themes are not tied to any specific major and are open to all.

This limited-choice model, with small, highly structured classes, was designed to provide high-touch teaching and clear student support for a population that has been traditionally underserved. Another unique feature of the program is the use of peer mentors and student success teams. The peer mentors were carefully selected from upperclassmen and then assigned to each of the eight sections of First-Year Seminar (two to three per theme). These peer mentors underwent specific training for their roles and were paid a stipend. Cohort-based student success teams were also designated for each of the themes and included a writing fellow, math tutor, library liaison, counseling intern, and digital learning specialist.

The purpose of this case report is to describe targeted student success and persistence efforts for first-year students in a new general education program using midterm grades and Save My Semester workshops.

Subjects

Based on data from fall 2014, the first cohort contained 242 students, who were predominantly female (64%) with an average age of 19.1 years. Blacks (60.3%) were the largest racial group, followed by White (15.7%), Hispanic (12%), unknown (8.3%), two or more (1.7%), and Asian (1.7%). They presented with financial need: 68.2% received a Pell Grant, 46.7% received state financial aid (MAP grant), and 65.7% had federal subsidized and unsubsidized loans.

Methods

The university implemented a variety of collaborative efforts to enhance student success and persistence among first-year students. These endeavors included intrusive advising, midterm grades, an academic recovery program, peer mentoring, and academic workshops. Intrusive advising is a vital part of student success. Key players such as the first-year adviser, peer mentors, faculty, and the Academic Resource Center staff communicate with each other to address student issues or opportunities and act accordingly. All of these partners interact with students on a weekly basis. During the fall 2014 semester, student affairs staff gathered midterm fall grades from learning community faculty (78% participation) to assess student progress. Through this initiative, it was reported that 42% of first-year students struggled academically. As a result, the Academic Resource Center implemented Save My Semester workshops that were held two weeks after midterm. The Save My Semester workshops helped students self-identify distractions and challenges, develop an action plan to get them back on track, and set goals and provided students with additional resources to be successful. Students performing below a C average were contacted by the Academic Resource Center staff and faculty to attend; 18% of all students attended.

In an effort to enhance student persistence, the Student Success Team, a cross-function committee, was established with the following members: the assistant vice president for student support services, the coordinator of new student programs and cohort adviser, the director of tutoring and academic support, and the residence hall director. The charge of the committee was to address students' needs; academic, faculty, and Prairie Place residence hall concerns; academic recovery; and to oversee the implementation of strategies to improve persistence. At the beginning of the spring 2015 semester, the Student Success Team implemented a Freshman First-Year Academic Recovery Program for all students placed on academic probation after their first semester. As part of this program, students on academic probation are required to

- participate in program with a signed contract outlining expectations;
- participate in weekly study tables;
- attend four student success workshops, including a writing workshop and Save My Semester;
- submit a fourth-week progress check to evaluate class performance; and
- submit a midterm progress check to report midterm grades.

Furthermore, all students were assigned an individual peer mentor and GSU resident students met every two weeks with designated faculty-in-residence who served as academic coaches.

Results

During preadvising appointments in October 2014, 143 freshmen completed an intake form as an estimate of their current grades. First-year students reported the following: 110 students (76.9%) indicated they were passing all of their courses, 22 students (15.4%) were not passing all of their classes, and 11 students (7.7%) were unsure if they were passing their courses. Despite the encouraging passing rates expected by 76.9% of the students, when final grades were submitted for the fall semester, 102 students (42%) of freshmen were placed on academic probation. The majority, 74 of those students (73%), did return to GSU in the second semester.

The Freshman First-Year Academic Recovery Program was implemented at the beginning of spring 2015 to address the needs of those 74 students. As a result, 71 academic recovery students (93%) participated in the program. Due to the structure and resources provided by the program, students' demeanor toward college and study habits changed. At the end of the spring semester, 78% of freshmen on academic probation raised their cumulative GPA, and 50% of freshmen were removed from academic probation.

GSU continues to assess student success and plans to expand and create new initiatives next fall, which will include early intervention strategies such as midterm grades recorded by faculty in the university's student information system (Colleague) and attendance tracking through Maxient software. GSU's academic recovery efforts will expand beyond freshmen to all lower-division academic recovery students. These students will be required to complete a Freshman/Sophomore Academic Recovery Program and be assigned a peer mentor or faculty coach, or both. In addition, all freshmen Prairie Place residents will be assigned a residence faculty coach to help students navigate through their first academic year. In addition, we will use our Learning Management Software (Blackboard) to create a specific place for information about academic recovery for general studies. Students will be able to connect with staff and resources online. Furthermore, a Learning Strategies workshop series will be piloted in the spring 2016 semester. Specific workshops will be offered related to topics identified as student needs in fall 2015.

Conclusion

This case describes one institution's efforts to provide targeted strategies to new freshmen using midterm grades and focused workshops to promote student success and persistence. We found that many students overestimated their performance in college courses and didn't recognize their risk for academic probation. Once they learned of that risk, those who participated in the many opportunities offered through the Academic Resource Center demonstrated improvements. The institution's awareness of student needs prompted specific, responsive action through mentoring, workshops, and study skills instruction. This just-in-time assessment was critical for changing the trajectory of the involved students.

The elements of this program are scalable to reach additional students. In fact, we have plans to nearly double the number of students reached next year as the program is extended to sophomores. We also have plans to expand the use of an early warning system and tracking through the use of electronic resources. The student needs are clear, and it is imperative that institutions address them as soon as possible to promote student success and persistence.

Note. Contributed by Amy V. Comparon, director of tutoring and academic support, Academic Resource Center; Ann M. Vendrely, associate provost and associate vice president of academic affairs; and Aurelio M. Valente, vice president of student affairs and dean of students, GSU. Used with permission.

Auburn University

Case 6.3 illustrates how an initial Auburn University project, the ePortfolio Project housed in the Office of University Writing, is now being expanded campus-wide, using an inclusive and collaborative cohort model—the Cohort ePortfolio. Faculty and staff from more than 40 different departments, programs, and support units across campus work together in learning communities. As departments opt into this large-scale commitment, they and their students receive on-time programming that supports the launch and sustained use of ePortfolios. Based on its earlier ePortfolio Project, the expanded Cohort ePortfolio is designed so that students and faculty monitor in real time students' progress toward achieving agreed-upon program- and institution-level outcomes. As described in Case 5.3 (pp. 134–135), faculty also refer students to previous learning documented in their ePortfolios to foster their abilities to draw from or integrate prior learning into current work. For their future lives, the Cohort ePortfolio showcases students' learning and also prepares them to be able to talk about their abilities and accomplishments to potential employers or graduate schools.

CASE 6.3.
Auburn University: Collaboration and Inclusivity in a Campus-Wide ePortfolio Project

The ePortfolio Project at Auburn University is a campus-wide initiative to support students as they create professional, outward-facing ePortfolios that showcase and synthesize their skills, knowledge, and abilities for an audience of potential employers or graduate schools. A natural outgrowth of our campus-wide writing initiative, the ePortfolio Project is Auburn's Quality Enhancement Plan (QEP) for the Southern Association of Colleges and Schools Commission on Colleges (SACSCOC) accreditation and is housed in the Office of University Writing. While the *products* that students create are meant to be "professional," the primary focus of the ePortfolio Project at Auburn is the *learning process* that occurs as students synthesize their curricular and cocurricular experiences to tell a coherent story about their education. Because of our focus on student learning—and because of the scale of our project—collaboration and inclusivity among faculty and staff are crucial.

The primary way the Office of University Writing engages faculty and staff and promotes collaboration and inclusivity in the ePortfolio Project is through the Cohort, which is essentially a learning community made up of small groups of faculty and staff from, currently, upward of 40 different departments, programs, and support units across campus. The Cohort represents a major difference between the ePortfolio Project and the writing initiative from which it grew: while the writing initiative certainly encourages collaboration and inclusivity, these values are built into the structure of the ePortfolio Project through the Cohort. Hallmarks of the Cohort include

- cross-disciplinary collaboration, including collaboration with student support units
- opt-in model—membership/participation is not mandatory; small groups of faculty and staff join when they decide ePortfolios make sense for their context
- flexible, responsive programming for faculty, staff, and students

Discussions among Cohort members often center on how to support current students' growth in the ePortfolio Project's four learning outcomes—critical thinking through reflection, effective communication, visual literacy, and technical competency. Working together with the Office of University Writing, the Cohort monitors student learning across disciplinary contexts in real time and creates action plans to respond quickly to what they observe. Examples of nimble responses include specialized workshops on reflective writing (for faculty and students), norming sessions for faculty who assess ePortfolios, workshops for faculty to learn the process of creating an ePortfolio, and the creation of a student workshop series for students who aren't enrolled in Cohort departments.

In an ePortfolio Project as large and multifaceted as ours, working toward scalability and coherence is a daily challenge that requires the kind of collaboration and inclusivity that the Cohort enables.

Note. Contributed by Lesley E. Bartlett, assistant director of the Office of University Writing, ePortfolio Project, Auburn University. Used with permission.

DePaul University

As Case 6.4 illustrates, DePaul University's, the Office for Teaching, Learning, and Assessment (TLA) has become the primary driver of real-time assessment, taking a multipronged approach and numerous steps to engage increasingly more individuals across the institution in assessment. This approach supports teaching and assessment as well as student learning to achieve the institution's goal of advancing more students to degree completion. Altogether, the approaches TLA has developed illustrate ways to continuously, as opposed to periodically, engage faculty and other constituencies in assessing their students' learning.

These approaches include inclusiveness and collaboration: multiple opportunities to learn more about and advance one's knowledge and practices in assessment with colleagues across the institution. In addition, TLA contributes to the institution's goal of advancing more students to graduation by providing information about learning resources to students, offering workshops and online resources to faculty about ways to provide early assessment of student achievement, and working with faculty and student peers to surround high-risk courses with supplemental instruction (SI) that supports those courses' outcomes.

CASE 6.4.

DePaul University: The Office for Teaching, Learning, and Assessment's Multipronged Approach on Many Fronts

Since its creation in 1999, DePaul University's Office for Teaching, Learning, and Assessment (TLA) has been guided by the belief that the dynamic and purposeful interplay of those three commitments provides a solid foundation that also helps the university meet its current vision statement, Vision 2018:

> The university will provide all students an academically challenging environment, consistently high-quality course offerings, and teaching excellence. DePaul is committed to the development of our faculty, ensuring they have the resources and capabilities to deliver an exemplary education; systems of institutional self-examination, assessment and benchmarking; optimal use of technology in support of teaching and learning; and continuing curricular innovation and program development to prepare students for an evolving, global society.

Specifically, the office's multipronged commitment to teaching, learning, and assessment is illustrated in Figure 6.4.1.

Figure 6.4.1. Structure and responsibilities of DePaul University's Office for Teaching, Learning, and Assessment.

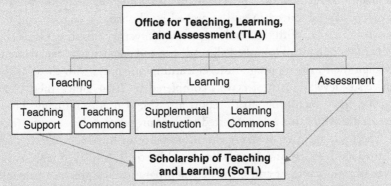

Support for Teaching

To support teaching, TLA regularly offers a series of faculty events that disseminate practical information about and research on teaching and learning through workshops, conferences, and forums offered annually in collaboration with other university partners, such as the writing center or the instructional technology office. These large-scale events often promote a particular teaching and learning concept, such as the scholarship of teaching and learning (SoTL) or civic engagement. To more effectively support a community of teacher-scholars at the university, the office created the Teaching and Learning Certificate Program (TLCP) (tlcp.depaultla.org), open to all faculty and instructional staff who are interested in enriching their teaching practices in collaboration with colleagues across the institution. TLCP workshops are led by faculty and instructional staff who cover topics focused on effective teaching and ways in which students learn. To receive a certificate, participants attend six events and create a digital teaching portfolio. Program participants share best practices, apply pedagogical strategies discussed at events to their teaching, and reflect in their portfolios on their development as teacher-scholars.

Support for Assessment

TLA has focused on four initiatives to engage more faculty and staff in a shared commitment to assessment. First, recognizing that buy-in and a sense of belonging are essential to engage faculty and others in assessment, in 2011 academic affairs led a university-wide process of revising the institution's learning goals and outcomes. This undertaking involved multiple constituencies from across the university working together to develop a first draft that was then reviewed by other constituencies, such as faculty council, student government, and academic affairs, before the revision was submitted to and approved by the faculty council and the provost in 2012. With the newly approved University Learning Goals and Outcomes in hand, TLA asked all academic and cocurricular departments to align their existing program-level learning outcomes with those at the university level. This project was completed in 2014. Since then DePaul has asked each program to report assessment results annually. These results are aggregated and presented to the campus.

Second, again recognizing the importance of buy-in, in 2013 TLA formed an Assessment Advisory Board. This board consists of representatives from all colleges and cocurricular programs and provides valuable advice to TLA on decisions about assessment procedures and processes. DePaul has noticed a marked increase in faculty and staff involvement in the assessment process, as well as in the quality of their commitment.

Third, identifying ways to recognize various individuals' commitment to assessment led TLA in 2014 to design a professional development/recognition program for faculty and staff engaged in assessment, the Assessment Certificate Program (acp.depaultla.org). The program has received an impressive welcome, with more than 100 faculty and academic staff already enrolled in the program, in addition to over 100 cocurricular staff members and 25 graduate students. This program consists of a series of workshops that faculty can attend individually (without pursuing the assessment certificate) or as a series of workshops that lead to an Assessment Certificate presented at our annual Teaching and Learning Conference. To receive a certificate, faculty/staff need to take an introduction to assessment workshop and four elective workshops (based on their own interests and needs), complete a culminating project of their choice, and attend a final workshop to present and discuss their culminating projects. This certificate program serves several purposes. First, DePaul builds capacity among its faculty and staff for engaging in the assessment of student learning. Second, TLA no longer holds all the assessment expertise: the accreditation requirements that inform assessment are not a mystery to the faculty and staff engaging in the assessment of student learning. Faculty and staff feel that there is purpose and support for the work they are doing with assessment. Finally, this program serves as a way to recognize faculty and staff engaging in the assessment of student learning.

The following year, TLA allocated part of its budget to assessment awards. DePaul already had awards for teaching and research, but no official recognition of assessment. To elevate the work of assessment to the level of faculty members' other responsibilities, DePaul felt it was important to recognize that work in a similar manner. DePaul now has two different assessment awards: the Spirit of Assessment Award, to recognize an individual who has made extraordinary efforts to promote a culture of assessment at DePaul University, and the Annual Assessment Award, to recognize the university group or unit presenting the best annual assessment report. The responsibility for these awards rests with the Assessment Advisory Board. Taken together, these initiatives have gone a long way to developing a true culture of assessment at DePaul.

Fourth, inspired by the university's broad definition of *research*, which includes developing methods that result in improving teaching and learning (see offices.depaul.edu/mission-and-values/about/Pages/Mission Statement.aspx), TLA developed a systematic plan to promote SoTL. That plan enables faculty to

- gain a practical understanding of what SoTL entails, become familiar with typical peer-review journals in their fields, and engage in productive discussions about relevant research articles;

- understand how SoTL directly connects to DePaul's mission—that is, to help faculty realize why and how students' learning can be meaningfully improved through SoTL;
- incorporate evidence-based effective teaching practices as they see fit in their own courses;
- contribute to SoTL by conducting research, namely classroom research activities, and publishing results in appropriate peer-review outlets; and
- pursue the university's formal value and recognition of SoTL in its merit reviews and promotion and tenure evaluations.

TLA and the Committee on Learning and Teaching (COLT), which directly reports to faculty governance (Faculty Council), developed a definition of *SoTL* and drafted a resolution asking the university faculty council to adopt the definition, endorse the full inclusion of SoTL in merit reviews and in promotion and tenure evaluations, and endorse the facilitation of SoTL by DePaul faculty and administrators through the same means used to support discipline-specific research and scholarship. Based on feedback from the Faculty Council, TLA and COLT revised the resolution. The endorsement of the revised version of the resolution was approved unanimously by the university Faculty Council on January 8, 2014.

Real-Time Student Learning Support

Under its umbrella of responsibilities, TLA also supports some of the university efforts aimed at enhancing the conditions for student learning so that more undergraduates complete their degrees. Two specific efforts are as follows:

1. The launch of a website featuring academic services under a unified brand (Success@DePaul; resources.depaul.edu/student-success).
   This centralized website links academic support services from across the university and offers students resources from orientation to graduation. For the first time, students can now learn about all the tutoring opportunities available at DePaul from one website. Students can also learn how to meet with their advisers, find career mentors, attend study sessions, and much more.
2. TLA engages faculty in integrating supplemental instruction (SI) into historically difficult courses. Peer-assisted study sessions in SI

are led by students known as SI Leaders. Faculty engagement and feedback help to inform the planning of SI sessions so that students can develop timely strategies for long-lasting and successful learning. The purposeful collaboration of TLA and faculty has been quite successful: over 90% of students who attend six or more SI sessions (over a nine-week period) have earned a C– or better in historically difficult courses.

Note. Contributed by Ruben D. Parra, director, Office for Teaching, Learning, and Assessment, DePaul University. Used with permission.

As these four case studies and others in this book illustrate, taking real-time student assessment to scale requires steadfastness of purpose, continuous staying power, and educators' and campus experts' on-the-ground resilience to respond to evidence of currently enrolled students' patterns of underperformance. The longer it takes institutions to take steps toward real-time assessment or to counter opposition to it, the more likely long-standing disparities in achievement and graduation rates will persist. As well, documented persistent gaps in students' achievement of relevant outcomes necessary for life and work, such as critical thinking, writing, problem-solving, or quantitative literacy, will remain.

Real-time student assessment is not a periodic commitment. It is not an add-on task or a service to the institution. It should not be driven primarily by external bodies. It should be internally driven by a shared commitment to our students' equitable achievement of high-quality degree- and program-level outcomes. It begins from the moment students log on to their first course, take a seat in their first classroom, transfer into or reenter our institutions—regardless of their education pathways. In the words of Carlow University, assessment is higher education's ethical commitment to our currently enrolled students. It takes place continuously in the present tense.

REFERENCES

Adelman, C., Ewell, P., Gaston, P., & Schneider, C. G. (2014, October). *The Degree Qualifications Profile 2.0: Defining U.S. degrees through demonstration and documentation of college learning.* Indianapolis, IN: Lumina Foundation. Retrieved from www.luminafoundation.org/dqp

Advisory Committee on Student Financial Assistance. (2012). *Pathways to success: Integrating learning with life and work to increase national college completion.* Washington, DC: Author. Retrieved from files.eric.ed.gov/fulltext/ED529485 .pdf

Aldrich, C. (2009a). *The complete guide to simulations & serious games: How the most valuable content will be created in the age beyond Gutenberg to Google.* San Francisco, CA: Pfeiffer.

Aldrich, C. (2009b). *Learning online with games, simulations, and virtual worlds: Strategies for online instruction.* San Francisco, CA: Jossey-Bass.

Alverno College. (2015). *The 8 core abilities.* Retrieved from www.alverno.edu/academics/ouruniquecurriculum/the8coreabilities

Alverno College. (n.d.). *Diagnostic Digital Portfolio.* Retrieved from www.alverno .edu/academics/ouruniquecurriculum/diagnosticdigitalportfolio/

American Historical Association. (2013). *AHA Tuning project: History discipline core.* Retrieved from www.historians.org/teaching-and-learning/current-projects/tuning/history-discipline-core

Arum, R., & Roksa, J. (2011). *Academically adrift: Limited learning on college campuses.* Chicago, IL: University of Chicago Press.

Arum, R., & Roksa, J. (2014). Let's ask more of our students—and of ourselves. *Chronicle of Higher Education.* Retrieved from chronicle.com/article/Lets-Ask-More-of-Our/148559/

Association of American Colleges & Universities. (2002). *Greater expectations: A new vision for learning as a nation goes to college.* Washington, DC: Author.

Association of American Colleges & Universities. (2005). *Liberal Education and America's Promise.* Washington, DC: Author. Retrieved from www.aacu.org/leap

Association of American Colleges & Universities. (2013). *LEAP employer-educator compact: Making quality a priority as Americans go to college.* Revised edition. Retrieved from https://aacu.org/sites/default/files/files/LEAP/compact.pdf

Association of American Colleges & Universities. (2014a). *VALUE: Valid assessment of learning in undergraduate education.* Retrieved from www.aacu.org/value

Association of American Colleges & Universities. (2014b, March). *Highlights from a three-year nine-state initiative on assessment and transfer.* Retrieved from www .aacu.org/sites/default/files/files/qc/QCHighlights2014.pdf

Association of American Colleges & Universities. (2015a, September 24). *Multi-state collaborative produces valuable evidence about writing, critical thinking, and quantitative literacy skills of undergraduate students using rubric-based assessment of students' authentic work.* Retrieved from www.aacu.org/press/press-releases/multi-state-collaboration-produces-valuable-new-evidence-about-writing-critical

Association of American Colleges & Universities. (2015b). *General education maps and markers: Designing meaningful pathways to student achievement.* Washington, DC: Author.

Association of American Colleges & Universities. (2016, November). *Bringing equity and quality learning together: Institutional priorities for tracking and advancing underserved students' success. Key findings from a survey and in-depth interviews among administrators at AAC&U member institutions.* Conducted on behalf of the Association of American Colleges & Universities by Hart Research Associates. Washington, DC: Author.

Association of American Colleges & Universities. (n.d.). *Integrating signature assignments into the curriculum and inspiring design.* Retrieved from www.aacu .org/sites/default/files/Signature-Assignment-Tool.pdf

Baum, S., & Flores, S. M. (2011, Spring). Higher education and children in immigrant families. *The Future of Children Publications, 21*(1), 171–193. Retrieved from http://www.futureofchildren.org/publications/journals/article/index.xml?jo urnalid=74&articleid=545files.eric.ed.gov/fulltext/EJ920372.pdf

Baum, S., Ma, J., & Payea, K. (2013). Education pays, 2013: The benefits of higher education for individuals and society. *The College Board.* Trends in Higher Education Series, 1–47. Retrieved from trends.collegeboard.org/sites/default/files/education-pays-2013-full-report.pdf

Betts, K. (2008, September). Online human touch (OHT) instruction and programming: A conceptual framework to increase student engagement and retention in online education. Part 1. *Merlot Journal of Online Learning and Teaching, 4*(3). Retrieved from jolt.merlot.org/vol4no3/betts_0908.pdf

Boyer, E. (1990). *Scholarship reconsidered: Priorities of the professoriate.* Princeton, NJ: Carnegie Foundation for the Advancement of Teaching.

Brusilovsky, P. (1999). Adaptive and intelligent technologies for web-based education. In C. Rollinger & C. Peylo (Eds.), *Künstliche Intelligenz, Special Issue on Intelligent Systems and Teleteaching, 4,* 19–25. Retrieved from citeseerx.ist.psu .edu/viewdoc/download?doi=10.1.1.16.5294&rep=rep1&type=pdf

Buckles, K., Hagemann, A., Malamud, O., Morrill, M. S., & Wozniak, A. K. (2013, July). *The effect of college education on health.* Working Paper No. 19222. Cambridge, MA: National Bureau of Economic Research. Retrieved from www .nber.org/papers/w19222

Cambridge, D. (2010). *Eportfolios for lifelong learning and assessment.* San Francisco, CA: Jossey-Bass.

Cambridge, D., Cambridge, B., & Yancey, K. (2009). *Electronic portfolios 2.0.* Sterling, VA: Stylus.

Campbell, J. P., DeBlois, P. B., & Oblinger, D. (2007). Academic analytics: A new tool for a new era. *EDUCAUSE Review, 42*(4), 40–57.

Carnevale, A. P., Smith, N., & Strohl, J. (2010). *Help wanted: Projections of jobs and education requirements through 2018*. Washington, DC: Georgetown University Center on Education and the Workforce. Retrieved from cew.georgetown.edu/wp-content/uploads/2014/12/fullreport.pdf

Carnevale, A. P., Smith, N., & Strohl, J. (2014, November). *Recovery: Job growth and education requirements through 2020*. Washington, DC: Georgetown University Center on Education and the Workforce. Retrieved from cew.georgetown.edu/report/recovery-job-growth-and-education-requirements-through-2020

Center of Inquiry in the Liberal Arts at Wabash College. (n.d.). *Research findings on the Wabash National Study of Arts Education, 2006–2012*. Retrieved from www.liberalarts.wabash.edu/study-research

Chen, H. and Light, T. (2010) *Electronic portfolios and student success: Effectiveness, efficiency, and learning*. Washington DC: Association of American Colleges & Universities.

Clark, R. C., & Mayer, R. E. (2003). *E-learning and the science of instruction*. San Francisco, CA: Pfieffer.

Complete College America. (2012, Spring). *Remediation: Higher education's bridge to nowhere*. Washington, DC: Author. Retrieved from www.completecollege.org/docs/CCA-Remediation-final.pdf

Complete College America. (n.d.). completecollege.org

Corcoran, T., Mosher, F. A., & Rogat, A. (2009). Learning progressions in science: An evidence-based approach to reform. Report RR-63. Philadelphia, PA: Consortium for Policy Research in Education.

Council on Adult and Experiential Learning. (2013, April 10). *Documenting competence: A learning portfolio*. Webinar. Retrieved from arkadinoneplacenh.adobeconnect.com/_a1008158243/p5m37zm3s8x/?launcher=false&fcsContent=true&pbMode=normal

Davila, A., & Mora, M. T. (2007, January). An assessment of civic engagement and educational attainment. *Fact Sheet*. Center for Information & Research on Civic Learning & Engagement. Retrieved from civicyouth.org/PopUps/FactSheets/FS_Mora.Davila.pdf

Desilver, D. (2014, January 15). College enrollment among low-income students still trails richer groups. *FactTank*. Pew Research Center. Retrieved from www.pewresearch.org/fact-tank/2014/01/15/college-enrollment-among-low-income-students-still-trails-richer-groups

DiCerbo, K. E., & Behrens, J. T. (2014). *The impact of the digital ocean on education*. White Paper. London: Pearson. Retrieved from research.pearson.com/digitalocean

Dietz-Uhler, B., & Hurn, J. E. (2013, Spring). Using learning analytics to predict (and improve) student success: A faculty perspective. *Journal of Interactive Online Learning, 12*(1), 17–26. Retrieved from www.ncolr.org/jiol/issues/pdf/12.1.2.pdf

Eberle-Sudre, K., Welch, M., & Nichols, A. H. (2015, December). *Rising tide: Do college grad rate gains benefit all students?* Washington, DC: Education Trust. Retrieved from edtrust.org/wp-content/uploads/2014/09/TheRisingTide-Do-College-Grad-Rate-Gains-Benefit-All-Students-3.7-16.pdf

Education and the Workforce Committee. (2014, July 7). *Advancing Competency-Based Education Demonstration Project Act.* Retrieved from edworkforce.house.gov/news/documentsingle.aspx?DocumentID=386869

Educause. (2015). *Next-generation learning challenges breakthrough models.* Retrieved from www.educause.edu/events/breakthrough-models-incubator

Ewell, P. T. (2013). *The Lumina Degree Qualifications Profile (DQP): Implications for assessment.* National Institute for Learning Outcomes Assessment. Retrieved from www.learningoutcomesassessment.org/documents/DQPop1.pdf

Eynon, B., & Gambino, L. (in press). *High-impact ePortfolio practice: A catalyst for student, faculty, and institutional learning.* Sterling, VA: Stylus.

Faber. S. (n.d). Positive effects of college degrees. *synonym.* Retrieved from classroom.synonym.com/positive-effects-college-degrees-4134.html

Fain, P. (2013, December 12). Competent at what? *Inside Higher Education.* Retrieved from www.insidehighered.com/news/2013/12/12/lumina-funded-group-seeks-lead-conversation-competency-based-education

Fain, P. (2014, October 28). Big ten and the next biggest thing. *Inside Higher Education.* Retrieved from www.insidehighered.com/news/2014/11/26/competency-based-bachelors-brandman-could-be-glimpse-future

Fain, P. (2015a, August 14). Defining college. *Inside Higher Education.* Retrieved from www.insidehighered.com/news/2015/08/14/aacus-moderate-strong-voice-competency-based-education-and-disruption

Fain, P. (2015b, September). Keeping up with competency. *Inside Higher Education.* Retrieved from https://www.insiderhighered.com/news/2015/09/10/amid-competency-based-education-boom-meeting-help-colleges-do-it-right

Federal Student Aid Office. (2013, March 19). *Applying for Title IV eligibility for direct assessment (competency-based) programs.* Retrieved from ifap.ed.gov/dpcletters/GEN1310.html

Federal Student Aid Office. (2014, July 31). *Experimental sites initiative.* Retrieved from experimentalsites.ed.gov/exp/approved.html

Felten, P., Gardner, J. N., Schroeder, C. C., Lambert, L. M., & Barefoot, B. O. (2016). *The undergraduate experience: Focusing institutions on what matters most.* San Francisco, CA: Jossey-Bass.

Ferris State University. (n.d.). *Small group instructional design.* Retrieved from www.ferris.edu/htmls/academics/center/services/sgid

Field, K. (2014, December 4). The talk—and pledges at the White House Summit on college opportunity. *The Chronicle of Higher Education.* Retrieved from chronicle.com/blogs/ticker/the-talk-and-pledges-at-the-white-house-summit-on-college-opportunity/90629

Finley, A., & McNair, T. (2013). *Assessing underserved students' engagement in high-impact practices.* Washington, DC: Association of American Colleges & Universities.

Ford, K. (2014, October). *Competency-based education: History, opportunities, and challenges.* Briefing Paper. UMUC Center for Innovation and Student Success. Retrieved from www.umuc.edu/innovatelearning/upload/cbe-lit-review-ford.pdf

Goffe, W. L., & Kauper, D. (2014). A survey of principles instructors: Why lecture prevails. *Journal of Economic Education, 45*(4), 360–375.

Greenstone, M., Looney, A., Patashnik, J., & Yu, M. (2013, June). *Thirteen economic facts about social mobility and the role of education.* Policy Memo. Hamilton Project. Washington, DC: Brookings Institution. Retrieved from www.brookings.edu/~/media/research/files/reports/2013/06/13-facts-higher-education/thp_13econfacts_final.pdf

Guetterman, T. C., & Mitchell, N. (2015). The role of leadership and culture in creating meaningful assessment: A mixed methods case study. *Innovative Higher Education.* Advance online publication. doi:10.1007/s10755-015-9330-y

Harper, S. R., & Associates. (2014). Succeeding in the city: A report from the New York City Black and Latino male high school achievement study. Philadelphia: University of Pennsylvania, Center for the Study of Race and Equity in Education. Retrieved from http://www.gse.upenn.edu/equity/nycReport

Harris, F., III, & Bensimon, E. M. (2007, Winter). The equity scorecard: A collaborative approach to assess and respond to racial/ethnic disparities in student outcomes. In *New Directions for Higher Education* 120. Special Issue: *Responding to the Realities of Race on Campus,* 77–84. San Francisco, CA: Jossey-Bass. Wiley Interscience. Retrieved from cue.usc.edu/tools/Harris_The%20Equity%20Scorecard.pdf

Hart Research Associates. (2013). *It takes more than a major: Employer priorities for college learning and student success.* Washington, DC: Association of American Colleges & Universities and Hart Research Associates. Retrieved from https://aacu.org/sites/default/files/files/LEAP/2013_EmployerSurvey.pdf

Hoxby, C., & Avery, C. (2013, Spring). The missing "one-offs": The hidden supply of high-achieving, low-income students. Economic Studies Program. *Brookings Papers on Economic Activity, 46*(1), 1–65.

Huizinga, J. (1955). *Homo ludens: A study of the play-element in culture.* Boston, MA: Beacon Press.

Humphreys, D., & Carnevale, A. (2016). *The economic value of liberal education* (Rev. ed.). PowerPoint. Retrieved from www.aacu.org/leap/economiccase

Hussar, W. J., & Bailey, T. M. (2011). *Projections of education statistics to 2020.* National Center for Education Statistics. Washington, DC: U.S. Government Printing Office. Retrieved from nces.ed.gov/pubs2011/2011026.pdf

Hutchings, P., Jankowski, N. A., & Schultz, K. E. (2016). Designing effective classroom assignments: Intellectual work worth sharing. *Change, 48*(1), 6–15.

Institute for Evidence-Based Change. (2012). *Tuning American higher education.* Encinitas, CA: Author.

Institute of International Education. (2014, November 17). *2014 open doors report.* Washington, DC: U.S. Department of State, Bureau of Educational and Cultural Affairs. Retrieved from www.iie.org/Research-and-Publications/Open-Doors

Jaschik, S. (2016, March 30). Grade inflation nation: Getting an A is really easier than ever. *Inside Higher Education*. Retrieved from www.slate.com/articles/life/inside_higher_ed/2016/03/grades_continue_to_steadily_rise_at_four_year_colleges.html

Justice, L. J., & Ritzhaupt, A. D. (2015). Identifying the barriers to games and simulations in education: Creating a valid and reliable survey instrument. *Journal of Educational Technology Systems, 44*(1), 86–125.

Kazin, K. (2015). *Blog.* Retrieved from collegeforamerica.org/cathrael-kazin-on-rigor-applicability-and-competencies-in-our-ba-degree

Kinzie, J., & Jankowski, N. (2015). Making assessment consequential: Organizing to yield results. In G. D. Kuh, S. O. Ikenberry, N. A. Jankowski, T. R. Cain, P. T. Ewell, P. Hutchings, & J. Kinzie (Eds.), *Using evidence of student learning to improve higher education* (pp. 113–136). San Francisco, CA: Jossey-Bass.

Klein-Collins, R. (2013, November). *Sharpening our focus on learning: The rise of competency-based approaches to degree completion.* Occasional Paper 20. Champaign, IL: National Institute for Learning Outcomes Assessment.

Kotkin, J. (2010, August). The changing demographics of America. *The Smithsonian*, 1–5. Retrieved from www.smithsonianmag.com/40th-anniversary/the-changing-demographics-of-america-538284

Kuh, G. D. (2008). *High-impact educational practices: What they are, who has access to them, and why they matter.* Washington, DC: Association of American Colleges & Universities. Retrieved from edtrust.org/wp-content/uploads/2013/10/PracticeGuide1.pdf

Kuh, G. D., Ikenberry, S. O., Jankowski, N., Cain, T. R., Ewell, P. T., Hutchings, P., & Kinzie, J. (2015). *Using evidence of student learning to improve higher education.* San Francisco, CA: Jossey-Bass.

Kuh, G. D., Jankowski, N., Ikenberry, S. O., & Kinzie, J. (2014). *Knowing what students know and can do: The current state of learning outcomes in US colleges and universities.* Urbana, IL: University of Illinois and Indiana University, National Institute for Learning Outcomes Assessment.

Kuh, G. D., Kinzie, J., Schuh, J. H., Whitt, E. J., & Associates. (2005/2010). *Student success in college: Creating conditions that matter.* San Francisco, CA: Jossey-Bass.

Kuh, G. D., O'Donnell, K., & Reed, S. (2013). *Ensuring quality and taking high-impact practices to scale.* Washington, DC: Association of American Colleges & Universities.

Lederman, D. (2015, September 25). Are they learning? *Inside Higher Education*. Retrieved from www.insidehighered.com/news/2015/09/25/new-effort-aims-standardize-faculty-driven-review-student-work

Levy, F., & Murnane, R. J. (2013). *Dancing with robots: Human skills for computerized work.* Next Report. Cambridge, MA: Third Way.

Little, B., & Arthur, L. (2010). Less time to study, less well prepared for work, yet satisfied with higher education: A UK perspective on links between higher education and the labour market. *Journal of Education and Work, 23*(3), 275–296.

Long, P. D., & Siemens, G. (2011). Penetrating the fog: Analytics in learning and education. *EDUCAUSE Review Online, 46*(95). Retrieved from www.educause .edu/ero/article/penetrating-fog-analytics-learning-and-education

Lumina Foundation. (2009, April 8). *Tuning USA: Lumina Foundation launches faculty-led process that will involve students and employers in linking college degrees to workplace relevance and students' mastery of agreed-upon learning objectives.* Retrieved from www.luminafoundation.org/news-and-events/tuning-usa-lumina-foundation-launches-faculty-led-process-that-will-involve-students-and-employers-in-linking-college-degrees-to-workplace-relevance-and-students-mastery-of-agreed-upon-learning-objectives

Lumina Foundation. (2011). *The Degree Qualifications Profile.* Indianapolis, IN: Author.

Lumina Foundation. (2013). *Competency-based education network.* Retrieved from www.cbenetwork.org

Lumina Foundation. (2014a). *Degree Qualifications Profile.* Retrieved from degree-profile.org/read-the-dqp/the-degree qualifications%20profile/intellectual-skills

Lumina Foundation. (2014b). *The degree qualifications profile 2.0.* Indianapolis, IN: Author.

Lumina Foundation. (2015). *Goal 2025.* Retrieved from luminafoundation.org/goal_2025

Lumina Foundation. (2016a, January). *Connecting credentials: Lessons from the national summit on credentialing and next steps in the national dialogue.* Indianapolis, IN. Retrieved from www.luminafoundation.org/files/resources/lessons-from-national-credentialing-summit.pdf

Lumina Foundation. (2016b, April). *A stronger nation: Postsecondary learning builds the talent that helps us rise.* Retrieved from strongernation.luminafoundation.org/report/2016

Maki, P. (2004). *Assessing for learning: Building a commitment across the institution.* Sterling, VA: Stylus.

Maki, P. (2015). *Assessment that works: A national call, a twenty-first-century response.* Washington, DC: Association of American Colleges & Universities.

Massachusetts Department of Higher Education. (2015). *What is the vision project?* Retrieved from www.mass.edu/visionproject/vision.asp

Masterson, K. (2013, May). *Giving MOOCs some credit.* American Council on Education. Retrieved from www.acenet.edu/the-presidency/columns-and-features/Pages/Giving-MOOCs-Some-Credit.aspx

Matthews, D., Zanville, H., & Duncan, A. G. (2016). *The emerging learning system: Report on the recent convening and new directions for action.* Indianapolis, IN: Lumina Foundation. https://www.luminafoundation.org/resources/the-emerging-learning-system

McCormick, A. C. (2003, Spring). Swirling and double-dipping: New patterns of student attendance and their implications for higher education. In *New Directions for Higher Education.* Special Issue: *Changing Student Attendance Patterns: Challenges for Policy and Practice.* Hoboken, NJ: John Wiley & Sons.

Michelson, E., & Mandell, A. (2004). *Portfolio development and the assessment of prior learning: Perspectives, models and practices* (2nd ed.). Sterling, VA: Stylus.

National Center for Education Statistics. (2005). Enrollment. *Fast Facts.* Washington, DC: U.S. Government Printing Office. Retrieved from nces.ed.gov/fastfacts/display.asp?id=98.

National Center for Education Statistics. (2010). *Status and trends in the education of racial and ethnic groups.* Washington, DC: U.S. Government Printing Office. Retrieved from nces.ed.gov/pubs2010/2010015/intro.asp

National Center for Education Statistics. (2011). *Digest of education statistics 2010.* Table 241: Percentage of first-year undergraduate students who took remedial education courses, by selected characteristics: 2003–04 and 2007–08. Washington, DC: U.S. Government Printing Office. Retrieved from nces.ed.gov/pubs2011/2011015.pdf

National Center for Education Statistics. (2012). *Higher education: Gaps in access and persistence study.* Washington, DC: U.S. Government Printing Office. Retrieved from nces.ed.gov/pubs2012/2012046.pdf

National Center for Education Statistics. (2013). *Digest of education statistics.* Table 376: Percentage of first-time full-time bachelor's degree–seeking students at four-year institutions who completed a bachelor's degree, by race/ethnicity, time to completion, sex, and control of institution: Selected cohort years, 1996 through 2005. Washington, DC: U.S. Government Printing Office. Retrieved from nces.ed.gov/programs/digest/d12/tables/dt12_376.asp

National Center for Education Statistics. (2015). *Digest of education statistics.* Table 326: Percentage of first-time full-time bachelor's degree–seeking students at four-year institutions who completed a bachelor's degree by race/ethnicity, time to completion, sex, and control of institution: Selected cohort years, 1996 through 2007. Washington, DC: U.S. Government Printing Office. Retrieved from nces.ed.gov/programs/digest/d14/tables/dt14_326.10.asp

National Institute for Learning Outcomes Assessment. (2016a). *Case studies of institutions using DQP and/or Tuning.* Retrieved from degreeprofile.org/case-studies

National Institute for Learning Outcomes Assessment. (2016b, May). *Higher education quality: Why documenting learning matters.* Urbana, IL: University of Illinois and Indiana University, Author.

National Institute for Learning Outcomes Assessment. (n.d.a). *Applications for participation in a charrette.* Retrieved from www.assignmentlibrary.org/uploaded/files/Charrette%20Call.pdf

National Institute for Learning Outcomes Assessment. (n.d.b). Assessment Library. Retrieved from www.assignmentlibrary.org

National Institute for Learning Outcomes Assessment. (n.d.c). DQP assignment library. Retrieved from www.assignmentlibrary.org/tags/542d60e149d860b30200000c

National Student Clearinghouse Research Center. (2012, November). *Completing college: A national view of student attainment rates.* A Signature Series Report 4. Retrieved from www.studentclearinghouse.info/signature/4/NSC_Signature_Report_4.pdf

National Student Clearinghouse Research Center. (2014, July). *Some college, no degree: A national view of students with some college enrollment but no completion.* Signature Report 7. Retrieved from nscresearchcenter.org/signaturereport7

Nellum, C. J., & Hartle, T. W. (2015, December). Federal watch: Where have all the low-income students gone? *Financial Aid.* American Council on Education. Retrieved from www.acenet.edu/the-presidency/columns-and-features/Pages/Federal-Watch-Where-Have-All-the-Low-Income-Students-Gone.aspx

Nichols, A. H., Eberle-Sudre, K., & Welch, M. (2016, March). *Rising tide II: Do Black students benefit as grad rates increase?* Washington, DC: Education Trust. Retrieved from edtrust.org/wp-content/uploads/2014/09/RisingTide_II.pdf

Organisation for Economic Co-operation and Development. (2012). *Education at a glance 2012: OECD indicators.* Embargoed copy. OECD Publishing. Retrieved from www.oecd.org/unitedstates/CN%20-%20United%20States.pdf

Organisation for Economic Co-operation and Development. (2014). *Education at a glance 2014: OECD indicators.* OECD Publishing. dx.doi.org/10.1787/eag-2014-en

PARFRAMEWORK. (2015). *University System of Maryland adopts PARFRAME-WORK to optimize statewide student success.* Retrieved from www.parframework.org/2015/10/usm-optimizes-statewide-student-success

Patten, E. (2012, February 21). Statistical portrait of the foreign-born population in the United States, 2010. *Hispanic Trends.* Pew Research Center. Retrieved from www.pewhispanic.org/2012/02/21/statistical-portrait-of-the-foreign-born-population-in-the-united-states-2010

Pew Research Center. (2014, February 11). The rising cost of not going to college. *Social and Demographic Trends.* Retrieved from www.pewsocialtrends.org/2014/02/11/the-rising-cost-of-not-going-to-college

Prescott, B. T., & Bransberger, P. (2012, December). *Knocking at the college door: Projections of high school graduates.* Boulder, CO: Western Interstate Commission for Higher Education. Retrieved from www.wiche.edu/info/publications/knocking-8th/knocking-8th.pdf

Prescott, B. T., & Bransberger, P. (2013, April). Demography as destiny: Policy considerations in enrollment management. *Policy Insights.* Boulder, CO: Western Interstate Commission for Higher Education. Retrieved from www.wiche.edu/pub/16709

Reilly, M. (2015). Getting genuine commitment for change. *Communications Skills for Leaders, 72*(7), 42–46. Retrieved from www.ascd.org/publications/educational-leadership/apr15/vol72/num07/Getting-Genuine-Commitment-for-Change.aspx

Reynolds, C., & Patten, J. (2014). *Leveraging the ePortfolio for integrative learning: A faculty guide to classroom practices for transforming student learning.* Sterling, VA: Stylus.

Rhodes, T. (2010). *Assessing outcomes and improving achievement: Tips and tools for using rubrics.* Washington, DC: Association of American Colleges & Universities.

Rhodes, T., & Finley, A. (2013). *Using the VALUE rubrics for improvement of learning and authentic assessment*. Washington, DC: Association of American Colleges & Universities.

Rodgers, M., Grays, M. P., Fulcher, K. H., & Jurich, D. P. (2012). Improving academic program assessment: A mixed methods study. *Innovative Higher Education, 38*, 383–395.

Schendel, E., & Macauley, W. J. (2012). *Building writing center assessments that matter*. Logan: Utah State University Press.

Schneider, C. G., & Schoenberg, R. (1999, March/April). Habits hard to break: How persistent features of campus life frustrate curricular reform. *Change, 31*(2), 30–35.

Small Group Instructional Diagnosis. (n.d.). Retrieved from depts.washington.edu/cidrweb/OLD/consulting/SGIDforms.pdf

Smith, N. (2013). *First-generation college students*. PowerPoint. Presented at CIC Leadership Development Meeting. Retrieved from www.cic.edu/News-and-Publications/Multimedia-Library/CICConferencePresentations/2014%20Walmart%20Symposium/First%20Generation%20College%20Students%20(Smith).pdf

Staklis, S., & Horn, L. (2012, July). New Americans in postsecondary education: A profile of immigrant and second-generation American undergraduates. *Stats in Brief*. National Center for Education Statistics. Washington, DC: U.S. Department of Education. Retrieved from nces.ed.gov/pubs2012/2012213.pdf

SUNY Empire State College. (n.d.). *The global learning qualifications framework*. Retrieved from www.esc.edu/suny-real/global-learning-qualifications-framework

Texas Higher Education Coordinating Board. (n.d.). *Tuning Texas through Lumina Foundation*. Retrieved from www.thecb.state.tx.us/index.cfm?objectid =B4B957B5-BD9D-A63B- 1C8FFEF251B26E00

Tinto, V. (2012). *Promoting student achievement one class at a time*. Retrieved from www.acenet.edu/news-room/Documents/Promoting-Student-Completion-One-Class-at-a-Time-Tinto.pdf

Tym, C., McMillion, R., Barone, S., & Webster, J. (2004, November). *First-generation college students: A literature review*. Texas Guaranteed Student Loan Corporation. Retrieved from www.tgslc.org/pdf/first_generation.pdf

Tyton Partners. (2015). *Learning to adapt: A case for accelerating adaptive learning in higher education*. Retrieved from tytonpartners.com/tyton-wp/wp-content/uploads/2015/01/Learning-to-Adapt-Case-for-Accelerating-AL-in-Higher-Ed.pdf

University Innovation Alliance. (n.d.). *Vision and prospectus*. Retrieved from www .theuia.org/sites/default/files/UIA-Vision-Prospectus.pdf

U.S. Department of Education. (2015, October 14). *Fact sheet: Department of Education launches the Educational Quality through Innovative Partnerships (EQUIP) experiment to provide low-income students with access to new models of education and training*. Retrieved from www.ed.gov/news/press-releases/fact-sheet-department-education-launches-educational-quality-through-innovative-partnerships-equip-experiment-provide-low-income-students-access-new-models-education-and-training

Vacarr, B. (2014, December 8). An aging America: Higher education's new frontier. *Chronicle of Higher Education.* Retrieved from chronicle.com/article/An-Aging-America-Higher/150425

Verba, S., Schlozman, K. L., & Brady, H. (1995). *Voice and equality: Civic voluntarism in American politics.* Cambridge, MA: Harvard University Press.

Watson, W. R., Yang, S., & Ruggiero, D. (2013). *Games in schools: Teachers' perceptions of barriers to game-based learning.* Association for Educational Communications & Technology. Annual Convention Proceedings.

Weinbaum, A., Rodriguez, C., & Bauer-Maglin, N. (2013, February). *Rethinking community college for the twenty-first century: The new community college at CUNY.* Funded with the support of the Bill & Melinda Gates Foundation. New York, NY: New Community College at CUNY. Retrieved from guttman.cuny.edu/wp-content/uploads/2015/05/NCCCaseStudylowres.pdf

White House. (2009, February 24). *Address to Joint Session of Congress.* Retrieved from www.whitehouse.gov/the_press_office/Remarks-of-President-Barack-Obama-Address-to-Joint-Session-of-Congress

White House. (2013, February 12). *Remarks by the president in the State of the Union Address.* The White House: Office of the Press Secretary. Retrieved from www.whitehouse.gov/the-press-office/2013/02/12/remarks-president-state-union-address

White House. (2014, January). Increasing college opportunity for low-income students: Promising models and a call to action. *White House Report.* Retrieved from www.luminafoundation.org/resources/increasing-college-opportunity-for-low-income-students

White House. (n.d.). *Education: Knowledge and skills for jobs of the future.* Retrieved from www.whitehouse.gov/issues/education/higher-education

Winkelmes, M., Copeland, D. E., Jorgensen, E., Sloat, A., Smedley, A., Pizor, P., . . . , & Jalene, S. (2015, May). Benefits (some unexpected) of transparently designed assignments. *The National Teaching & Learning Forum, 24*(4), 4–6.

Yeado, J. (2013, July 17). *Intentionally successful: Improving minority student college graduation rates.* Washington, DC: Education Trust. Retrieved from edtrust.org/wp-content/uploads/2013/10/Intentionally_Successful.pdf

Yeado, J., Haycock, K., Johnstone, R., & Chaplot, R. (2014, January). *Education Trust higher education guide: Learning from high-performing and fast-gaining institutions.* Washington, DC: Education Trust. Retrieved from edtrust.org/wp-content/uploads/2013/10/PracticeGuide1.pdf

Also available from Stylus

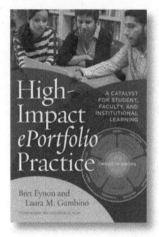

High-Impact ePortfolio Practice
A Catalyst for Student, Faculty, and Institutional Learning
Bret Eynon and Laura M. Gambino
Foreword by George D. Kuh

Drawing on the campus ePortfolio projects developed by a constellation of institutions that participated in the Connect to Learning network, Eynon and Gambino present a wealth of data and revealing case studies. Their broad-based evidence demonstrates that, implemented with a purposeful framework, ePortfolios correlate strongly with increased retention and graduation rates, broadened student engagement in deep learning processes, and advanced faculty and institutional learning.

The core of this book presents a comprehensive research-based framework, along with practical examples and strategies for implementation, and identifies the key considerations that need to be addressed in the areas of Pedagogy, Professional Development, Outcomes Assessment, Technology, and Scaling Up.

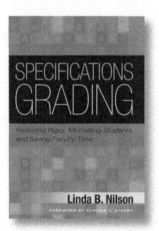

Specifications Grading
Restoring Rigor, Motivating Students, and Saving Faculty Time
Linda Nilson
Foreword by Claudia J. Stanny

"What a ridiculously simple yet profound plan for achieving what Nilson purports. Imagine, students demonstrating mastery of skill for a grade! Students taking back ownership of their progress! Students becoming our clients rather than our customers! Specs grading, get ready to sashay in and partner up with the outcomes that grades should really reflect."
—**Carol Washburn**, *Senior Instructional Designer, Manager, Teaching & Learning Center for Instructional Development & Distance Education, University of Pittsburgh*

"This book will change your life! Every instructor should buy it now. Nilson shows us how to make grading easier, more logical, and more consonant with research on learning and motivation. A practical, time-saving, student-motivating system of grading. A major advance in our thinking about how we grade and how students learn."—**Barbara Walvoord**, *Professor Emerita, University of Notre Dame*

22883 Quicksilver Drive
Sterling, VA 20166-2102

Subscribe to our e-mail alerts: www.Styluspub.com